EYE ON
ART

Claude Monet
Founder of French Impressionism

By Danielle Haynes

Portions of this book originally appeared in *Claude Monet* by Stuart A. Kallen.

LUCENT
PRESS

Published in 2019 by
Lucent Press, an Imprint of Greenhaven Publishing, LLC
353 3rd Avenue
Suite 255
New York, NY 10010

Designer: Deanna Paternostro
Editor: Melissa Raé Shofner

Library of Congress Cataloging-in-Publication Data

Names: Haynes, Danielle, author.
Title: Claude Monet : founder of French impressionism / Danielle Haynes.
Description: New York : Lucent Press, 2019. | Series: Eye on art | Includes
  bibliographical references and index.
Identifiers: LCCN 2018016330 (print) | LCCN 2018016783 (ebook) | ISBN
  9781534565302 (eBook) | ISBN 9781534565296 (library bound book) | ISBN
  9781534565289 (pbk. book)
Subjects: LCSH: Monet, Claude, 1840-1926. | Painters–France–Biography. |
  Impressionism (Art)–France.
Classification: LCC ND553.M7 (ebook) | LCC ND553.M7 H39 2019 (print) | DDC
  759.4–dc23
LC record available at https://lccn.loc.gov/2018016330

Printed in the United States of America

CPSIA compliance information: Batch #BW19KL: For further information contact Greenhaven Publishing LLC, New York, New York at 1-844-317-7404.

Please visit our website, www.greenhavenpublishing.com. For a free color catalog of all our high-quality books, call toll free 1-844-317-7404 or fax 1-844-317-7405.

Contents

Foreword

What is art? There is no one answer to that question. Every person has a different idea of what makes something a work of art. Some people think of art as the work of masters such as Leonardo da Vinci, Mary Cassatt, or Michelangelo. Others see artistic beauty in everything from skyscrapers and animated films to fashion shows and graffiti. Everyone brings their own point of view to their interpretation of art.

Discovering the hard work and pure talent behind artistic techniques from different periods in history and different places around the world helps people develop an appreciation for art in all its varied forms. The stories behind great works of art and the artists who created them have fascinated people for many years and continue to do so today. Whether a person has a passion for painting, graphic design, or another creative pursuit, learning about the lives of great artists and the paths that can be taken to achieve success as an artist in the modern world can inspire budding creators to pursue their dreams.

This series introduces readers to different artistic styles, as well as the artists who made those styles famous. As they read about creative expression in the past and present, they are challenged to think critically about their own definition of art.

Quotes from artists, art historians, and other experts provide a unique perspective on each topic, and a detailed bibliography is provided as a starting place for further research. In addition, a list of websites and books about each topic encourages readers to continue their exploration of the fascinating world of art.

This world comes alive with each turn of the page, as readers explore sidebars about the artistic process and creative careers. Essential examples of different artistic styles are presented in the form of vibrant photographs and historical images, giving readers a comprehensive look at art history from ancient times to the present.

Art may be difficult to define, but it is easy to appreciate. In developing a deeper understanding of different art forms, readers will be able to look at the world around them with a fresh perspective on the beauty that can be found in unexpected places.

Leading a Movement

Leonardo da Vinci, Pablo Picasso, and Salvador Dalí have come to be known as the finest examples of the periods of art they were a part of—the Italian Renaissance, Cubism, and Surrealism, respectively. Additionally, it is not an exaggeration that Claude Monet is perhaps the single greatest contributor and the most well-known innovator of the Impressionism movement. The very word—Impressionism—was cemented into the art world's vocabulary by one of Monet's earliest examples of the technique: *Impression, Sunrise.*

What associated Monet with Impressionism was how he looked at the world. When he went for a walk in the woods or took a stroll along the beach,

he glanced here and there like most people do. He gathered impressions of the landscape but rarely looked closely at the fine details of the scene before him. Unlike most people, however, Monet had the skill, talent, and creative drive to put these fleeting glimpses, or impressions, on canvas with brush and paint. Monet summed up his way of seeing while giving advice to an artist friend: "When you go out to paint, try to forget what objects you have before you, a tree, a house, a field or whatever ... merely think here is a little square of blue, here is an oblong of pink, here is a streak of yellow, and paint it just as it looks to you, the exact color and shape, until it gives you your own naïve

Monet enjoyed painting outside and later in life focused his attention on the gardens surrounding his home in Giverny, France.

impression of the scene before you."[1]

Monet was the leader of this revolutionary style, which was also practiced by renowned artists such as Édouard Manet, Paul Cézanne, Edgar Degas, Camille Pissarro, and Pierre-Auguste Renoir. The term Impressionism was first used in 1874 by a critic who wrote a review of Monet's paintings at an exhibition.

For most of his life, Monet struggled financially and was beset with many personal problems. He had a disapproving father and a sick wife, and lost a close friend and patron in the Franco-Prussian War. He also struggled in his career as the style he pioneered and loved so much went in and out of fashion as tastes changed and new artists gained favor with the critics. In fact, until he was 40 years old, Monet's talent for capturing momentary impressions on canvas with quick, flickering brushstrokes was widely mocked and disapproved of by those in the elite world of French art.

Despite many setbacks in his personal and professional life, Monet continued to place strong demands on himself. He never stopped believing in the power of art to express ideas and transform the spirit. This may be confirmed by his incredible output of more than 2,500 paintings that radically altered the way art was understood and created. Today, Monet's works are sold for tens of millions of dollars.

Monet abandoned the studio to work *en plein air*, or in the open air. He took joy in painting outside in all types of weather, even during howling storms on the French coast. Casting aside the formal painting methods of earlier artists, Monet created art *sur le motif*, or on the spot. By doing so, he invented a unique way of viewing nature as a spontaneous, transient world of ever-changing light and color. As curator and leading Impressionist scholar Charles F. Stuckey explained, "[Monet] specialized in paintings of uncommonly brilliant light, in which physical objects dematerialize into fantasies. These works extend the original goals of Impressionism from [ordinary] pictorial journalism to meditative nature poetry."[2] Monet referred to these images as *féerique*, or fairy-tale-like.

During the second half of Monet's life, audiences finally recognized his genius. He became celebrated by the French people. Today, his home and gardens in Giverny, France, where he created so many of his paintings, are a national monument. They are listed among such famous French landmarks as the Eiffel Tower and the Arc de Triomphe in tour guides. The main street running through Giverny is named Rue Claude Monet.

In the 20th century, Monet's work influenced artists who painted styles such as Cubism, Surrealism, and Abstract Expressionism. Thus, Monet laid the foundations for modern art while creating unmatched visions of beauty that are among some of the most popular fine art images in the world today.

CHAPTER ONE

Childhood in Le Havre

Oscar-Claude Monet was born November 14, 1840, to Claude-Adolphe and Louise-Justine Aubrée Monet. Though Oscar, as his parents called him, spent his first five years in the French capital of Paris, his earliest memories as a child were of the city of Le Havre, located on France's northern Normandy coast. A major port town, Le Havre's nearness to the sea, beaches, and the River Seine inspired the young artist, who would grow up to be the city's most renowned resident.

In 1845, Monet's family moved to Le Havre, where his aunt, Marie-Jeanne Lecadre, and her husband owned a wholesale grocery and ship supplier business. The Lecadres were prosperous and owned a large villa near the sea where they hosted parties and musical concerts. Though they were successful in their business, they often took in boarders at their home to supplement their income.

In Le Havre, Monet's father purchased a house next to the harbor. This gave young Monet views of nearby resort hotels, a beach, and a bay filled with hundreds of sailboats. Monet later captured this scene in his 1867 painting *Garden at Sainte-Adresse*, which featured his father watching ships sail past while sitting in a beautiful garden.

In his caricature sketches, such as Léon Manchon, *shown here, Monet exaggerated the features of people he saw.*

Seaside Caricatures

Despite the nostalgia portrayed in *Garden at Sainte-Adresse*, Monet's father and uncles were conservative businessmen who hated the arts and had little use for painters. They encouraged young Monet to ignore his artistic side and instead study business. However, Monet had an intense dislike of school, which he called prison. He ignored his lessons in Latin, Greek, grammar, and math and spent his days doodling, drawing cartoons of his teachers in his notebooks. Monet was more interested in the art and drawing lessons he received from Jacques-François Orchard, who had been a student of the famed French painter Jacques-Louis David. As soon as the school day ended, Monet escaped to the nearby beaches, cliffs, and ocean waters. He later recalled that as a child he thought, "I should like to be always near [the sea] or on it ... and when I die, to be buried in a buoy."[3]

Little else is known about Monet's early life until his artistic career began in 1856. At the age of 16, he began sketching charcoal caricatures—cartoonlike drawings with exaggerated features—of local dignitaries and tourists dressed in their best vacation clothes. Pictures such as *Caricature of Léon Manchon* are typical of Monet's style at the time. In the drawing, Manchon has an oversize head, a huge nose, long sideburns curling down his cheeks, sticklike legs, and tiny feet.

The sketches were so inventive, humorous, and expertly drawn that they caught the eye of a local merchant who sold art supplies in a shop called Gravier's, located on Le Havre's fashionable Paris Street. Every Sunday morning, Gravier's placed a new batch of Monet's drawings in the shop window where appreciative crowds gathered to see who the young artist was mocking that week. The cartoons quickly sold for 15 to 20 francs each, giving the 16-year-old artist a weekly income equal to about $500 in today's money. "Had I carried on," Monet later remarked, "I would have been a millionaire."[4]

Boudin, the Mentor

Monet's caricatures were often displayed in Gravier's shop window alongside moody seascape and landscape paintings by Eugène Boudin, a 32-year-old artist who occasionally worked at the shop. Boudin painted outdoors, what the French called *en plein air*. He believed that canvases produced in the open air had a power and energy that could not be matched by images created in a studio.

At the time, the idea of painting outdoors was a relatively new concept, made easy and convenient by various artistic innovations in the mid-19th century. In earlier years, painters had to create their own pigments from minerals, plants, and animal parts, and mix them with oils

A Forceful Personality

Monet's strong personality became apparent at an early age. In this portrait by Pierre-Auguste Renoir, the artist is shown at work.

1. William C. Seitz, *Claude Monet*. New York, NY: Harry N. Abrams, 1982, p. 11.

Monet was known for his sometimes overbearing personality, even at an early age, as William C. Seitz wrote in *Claude Monet*:

Most of the traits that were to make Monet a great painter were manifested early ... [He] was not religious—indeed, he had little faith in anything that was not drawn from direct experience. He was persistent, had small need for social approval, and was stimulated by both hostility and adversity: "Without my dear Monet, who gave courage to all of us," [Impressionist artist Pierre-Auguste] Renoir once recalled, "we would have given up!" But not all his traits were equally admirable ...

Though willing to endure any degree of discomfort for his art, Monet was never to lose a taste for the overindulgent pattern of French middle-class life. He ate, it is said, like four men; he could be taciturn [reserved] and snappish, had a tendency toward vindictiveness, and exhibited a shameless craftiness where money and the sale of pictures were concerned. By the time he was sixteen he showed unmistakable talent, but he turned it to making caricature portraits at twenty francs a sitting.[1]

in a studio environment. In 1800, however, bright new oil paints were sold in portable tin tubes for the first time. These paints were easy to use outdoors and were eagerly adopted by painters throughout Europe and the United States.

Boudin took full advantage of such artistic advancements. After seeing Monet's expert caricatures, he convinced the young man to accompany him on a painting excursion to nearby Rouelles, France. Upon seeing Boudin open his French easel and begin painting *en plein air*, Monet was deeply moved: "Suddenly a veil was torn away. I had understood—I had realized what painting could be. By the single example of this painter devoted to his art with such independence, my destiny as a painter opened out to me."[5]

The first drawings Monet made on outings with Boudin were created between July and September 1856. They consisted of a number of pencil sketches of scenery, sailing vessels, and local fishermen, gardeners, and children. The subject matter was simple, but the quality of Monet's drawings at this time reveal talents beyond those of the average young artist. During this period, Monet also worked in color, using crayons of powdered pigment called pastels to create village scenes and seascapes. These works reveal that Monet was already a skilled artist by this time. The details and the distinct contrasts between shadows and light show a professional touch that he had obviously been nurturing for a number of years.

The Barbizon School

Early on, Monet chose to depict scenes in nature. This set him apart from many local artists who were painting the modern buildings, railroads, and bustling ports built during Le Havre's rapid expansion after 1840. Describing the area, French writer and critic Jules Janin said that Le Havre was "the industrial warehouse for the entire world [and] the crossroads of all industrial products ... [with] few remarkable monuments ... [and] the most beautiful sugar refineries [and] construction yards in the region."[6] While these monuments to production were within easy walking distance of Monet's home, the young artist chose to visit the fields, forests, and shores as yet untouched by the swift development.

Monet's choice of subject matter was undoubtedly influenced by the Barbizon school of painting that was active at the time. The Barbizon school was not a learning institution but a group of people who

Monet's early focus on nature in his paintings was influenced by the Barbizon school. Shown here is *View at Rouelles, which was painted in 1858.*

shared a similar artistic philosophy and style. It was named for the rustic village of Barbizon near the wild and beautiful Forest of Fontainebleau located about 40 miles (64 km) from Paris.

The rural community attracted painters such as Jean-François Millet and Camille Flers, who were inspired by Barbizon's natural fields and forests untouched by human hands. Barbizon art also had a political aspect as the painters portrayed farmers, hunters, gravediggers, and other workers going about their daily tasks. These paintings were meant to show the common person as someone worthy of admiration, as opposed to the politicians, nobility, and military leaders who were romanticized by France's most popular artists at the time.

The Barbizon painters later provided a strong influence for the Impressionists, but in the 1850s their art was a commercial failure. It was rejected by the influential Académie des Beaux-Arts (Academy of Fine Arts), which held an annual or biannual exhibition called the Salon. Any artist who hoped for success had to be accepted by the Salon, and those who were not accepted often stopped painting. Some even committed suicide.

As outsiders, the Barbizon painters held their own small art shows and lived the lives of poor, struggling artists. It is impossible to say if Monet was aware of the hardships faced by this school of nature artists, but he began to spend less time painting in the open air to pursue commercial success with his caricatures. Between 1856 and 1859, the young artist created dozens of satirical drawings, about 60 of which still survive.

Moving to Paris

In 1857, Monet's mother died. Her sister, whom Monet called Aunt Lecadre, took over his care and upbringing. As an amateur artist herself, Lecadre encouraged Monet to continue painting, even as his father insisted he continue his schooling to become a businessman. After his final exams, however, Monet announced his intention to move to Paris and become a professional artist. Describing the attraction to the big city, Paul Hayes Tucker wrote, "As the cultural capital of Europe and the center of artistic production and exchange in France, Monet knew it was where he could get serious training and be able to see significant art in abundance."[7]

Lecadre knew several painters who exhibited at the Salon des Beaux-Arts, and she convinced Monet's father to allow his son to move to Paris. With a letter of introduction from his Aunt Lecadre, Monet visited Barbizon landscape painter Constant Troyon, a family friend. After viewing Monet's work, Troyon made his recommendations: Monet should first attend the École des Beaux-Arts (School of Fine Arts), run by the Académie des Beaux-Arts, followed by a summer of painting *en plein air* in Le Havre, with a return to school in autumn. Lecadre and Monet's father agreed to provide a steady allowance as long as Monet followed Troyon's plan.

By the spring of 1859, Monet was in Paris, joyously exploring the sprawling art markets. Writing to Boudin, he excitedly described the landscape paintings by Troyon, Charles-François Daubigny, and Camille Corot as beautiful, marvelous, and astonishing. The 18-year-old Monet also criticized respected painters. He described a seascape by Eugène Isabey as "a horrible, huge picture," and a landscape by Jean-Louis Hamon as "a terrible thing ... It's hypocritical and pretentious. In a word he knows nothing about nature."[8]

Training at the Académie Suisse

In February 1860, Monet decided the best place to pursue both his artistic and business-related interests would be a small rented studio in Montmartre, a hilly district that was the artistic center of Paris. Rather than attend the respected École des Beaux-Arts, Monet chose the Académie Suisse, a much less formal art school run by painter Charles Suisse. Such small, independent schools were places where students learned directly from established masters, whose work had been accepted by the Salon. Most students attended these schools hoping to receive enough training to pass the difficult entrance exam into the École, but Monet was attracted to the easygoing atmosphere of the academy.

At the Académie Suisse, the schedules were flexible. No exams or formal critiques of student work were given, and the teachers were down-to-earth artists rather than professors such as those found at the École. As author Sue Rose explained, the Académie Suisse was a perfect setting for Monet, who had long been uncomfortable in academic settings:

The studio was large, bare, well lit, with two windows, one overlooking the courtyard, the other looking out across the river. The walls were grimy with smoke, and completely empty except for the easels and the models' metal crossbar, with its ropes and nooses used [by the model to maintain their stance while holding the] most difficult poses. The students shouted across to one another, teased the model, and puffed on their pipes, sending smoke up to the ceiling. Monet, though outgoing and popular, studied contentiously, working with great concentration.[9]

The relaxed setting at the Académie

Salon des Refusés

Salon des Refusés was only officially held three times—in 1863, 1864, and 1873—it did much to organize and inspire artists who would come to be known as Impressionists. Art historian Albert Boime wrote in 1970:

> From the time of the second Salon des Refusés to the first Impressionist exhibition of 1874—exactly one decade later—the idea of the Salon des Refusés kept alive the hope of combating despotic [undemocratic] juries and encouraged the aspirations of progressive artists. It became a rallying point for the Impressionists, instilling in them a certain sense of security and inspiring a collaborative effort to an extent heretofore unknown in the history of independent French art. While the Impressionists continued to seek recognition through the official system, the Salon des Refusés provided them with a model of group participation and sustained their revolutionary attitude.[1]

1. Albert Boime, "The Salon des Refusés and the Evolution of Modern Art," *Art Quarterly*, Spring 1970, p. 416. www.albertboime.com/Articles/12.pdf.

Suisse had attracted an earlier generation of rebellious artists, and the school's alumni included renowned painters such as Eugène Delacroix, Honoré Daumier, and Gustave Courbet. During his year at the school, Monet befriended several students who would themselves become famous, including Impressionist painters Camille Pissarro, Armand Guillaumin, and Paul Cézanne.

Military Career

In 1861, Monet was drafted into the military. At the time, wealthy men could buy their way out of the service, and Monet's father offered to pay for his son's discharge on the condition that he return to Le Havre and work in the family business. Monet refused and instead signed up for a 7-year term in a cavalry division called the First Regiment of African Light Cavalry. With dreams of finding adventure in Africa, Monet shipped out to Algeria. Within one year, however, he contracted typhoid fever (a disease that includes symptoms such as stomach pains, weakness, fever, and loss of appetite) and was sent home on extended sick leave.

Back in Le Havre, the 22-year-old Monet painted nonstop. Meanwhile, Aunt Lecadre, always seeking to help her nephew, offered to buy him out of the army at a cost of

3,000 francs, a large sum that could have supported a typical French family for a year. However, both Lecadre and Monet's father insisted that no more money would be forthcoming unless Monet returned to Paris to study with a recognized teacher. He consented and was soon back in Paris under the guardianship of painter Auguste Toulmouche, a friend of his aunt's who had recently won a medal for his work in the annual Salon exhibition.

Toulmouche studied Monet's paintings and recommended he study with Charles Gleyre. Like Charles Suisse, Gleyre ran a tolerant school and encouraged artists to express their individuality. During his 18 months at the school, Monet befriended several students including Frédéric Bazille—the son of a wealthy doctor who was studying medicine as well as art. Bazille held Monet in great esteem and would help him out of financial difficulties for many years. Pierre-Auguste Renoir was also a student at Gleyre's, and he, Bazille, Alfred Sisley, and Monet formed bonds of friendship that would last throughout their lives.

Traditional Ideals

By 1864, Monet was finished with school and was pursuing life as a Parisian artist. He painted landscapes in the Forest of Fontainebleau and traveled to the Normandy coast to paint seascapes with Bazille. Before long, the two men were sharing a studio, and both were preparing paintings to submit to the Salon in March 1865. Monet's canvases depicted two seascapes: one of the Seine estuary, the other a view of the coast near Sainte-Adresse, a small town near Le Havre.

The annual Salon exhibition was incredibly important in the art world. It was attended by some of the most influential artists and art buyers in the world, and it was the cause of great anxiety for thousands of French painters. As important as the Salon was, it was also traditional and old-fashioned. The judges of the Salon jury were famously unadventurous. As Jim Lane explained, "It would be hard to imagine a more conservative gaggle of immobile, stodgy [old-fashioned], establishment, stick-in-the-mud hacks bent upon cementing their high and mighty academic traditions in the minds of the public and artists alike, or a group of so-called 'art experts' in the press corps more dedicated to aiding and abetting this effort."[10]

This art establishment was merciless upon those who did not conform to its traditionalist ideas. For example, the 1863 Salon had been exceptionally brutal, rejecting the now-famous painting *Luncheon on the Grass* by Édouard Manet. The jury considered the depiction of a nude woman at a picnic to be vulgar and thought Manet's use of sharply contrasting tones and colors too experimental. The jury also rejected innovative works by Bazille, Sisley, and others. This caused uproar in the arts community that might be compared to someone's chosen presidential candidate losing in modern times.

The rejections and subsequent outrage led President Napoleon III to command the creation of the Salon des Refusés, a counter-exhibition for those artists whose works had been rejected by the Salon.

Success at the Salon

Monet submitted to the Salon for the first time in 1865—and two of his paintings were accepted. *Mouth of the Seine at Honfleur* and *La Pointe de la Hève at Low Tide* were seascapes unlike the paintings Monet was known for at the time. In these paintings, Monet used more subdued colors and traditional perspective and composition.

However, as art scholar and museum curator William C. Seitz wrote, the paintings show artistic touches unique to Monet:

> [The] skies are cloud-filled and the atmospheric tone ... is silvery. The hues are not brilliant, but the sparkle and movements of the shore are nevertheless captured by the

spontaneity of the brushwork, which varies from one passage to another. The beaches are often built up of crisp touches [of the brush], or even dotted, for they are in fact not sandy but com-

posed of sea-rounded pebbles in a [number] of tones. Monet's quick brush also adapted itself to the chop of open water, the pound of surf, or, heavily loaded [with paint], to banks of clouds.[11]

Despite the success of his seascapes in the Salon, Monet returned to nontraditional techniques. He began work on his own take on Manet's *Luncheon on the Grass*, which he intended to submit for the

Monet's 1865 submissions to the Salon were more traditional than his normal style. Shown here is La Pointe de la Hève at Low Tide.

1866 Salon. Though Monet spent much of his time in 1865 and 1866 preparing sketches and painting the large canvas—15 feet by 20 feet (4.5 m by 6 m)—he never finished it.

In 1920, Monet said that the painting fell victim to his financial woes of the time, writing, "I had to pay my rent, I gave it to the landlord as security and he rolled it up and put in the cellar. When I finally had enough money to get it back, as you can see, it had gone mouldy."[12]

When Monet was able to get the painting back in 1884, he cut it up and kept three pieces, one of which has since disappeared. Though it remained unfinished, critics considered Monet's take on *Luncheon on the Grass* revolutionary. It depicted ordinary subject matter—a picnic—with no dominant subject to draw the eye. Monet captured a spontaneous moment in time—a woman touches her hair, another sets down a plate. In doing so, he took the art of painting in a new direction that would someday be imitated by thousands of artists throughout the world.

CHAPTER TWO

Introduction of a Muse

After abandoning the massive *Luncheon on the Grass*, Monet decided to enter two other more conservative paintings in the 1866 Salon. The first painting, *The Road from Chailly to Fontainebleau*, is a landscape Monet painted in 1864 near the village of Fontainebleau.

The second, *Camille (The Woman in the Green Dress)*, reused a model from *Luncheon*. This model would become a familiar face in Monet's paintings over the next 15 years. The painting was a life-size portrait of Camille Doncieux, Monet's future wife. Monet completed the canvas in four days right before the Salon deadline. It was praised for the artist's use of color, the contrast of the dark green satin of the gown and Camille's pale skin.

Commenting on the pose and the artist's treatment of the subject, Rose wrote, "The 'finish' of the textures — silk and fur, skin and hair — and the delicacy of her long, pale fingers, made this [painting] the epitome of an acceptable work. This was how the bourgeois audience wanted to see their women in art."[13]

The Salon accepted both paintings, and the praise for *Camille* sparked an interest in Monet's work. He received multiple commissions and sold several older paintings on the heels of the exhibition.

Camille (The Woman in the Green Dress) *was a life-size portrait of Monet's future wife, Camille Doncieux. Monet submitted the painting to the 1866 Salon exhibition to much acclaim.*

For Monet, the 1866 Salon exhibition was a triumph, but the achievement had a troubling aspect. Camille Doncieux was still in her teens when Monet immortalized her on canvas. She was attractive, intelligent, and came from a wealthy family. However, Camille and Monet began living together without getting married, which was considered scandalous, and both of their families cut off financial support. This created a major rift between Monet and his father, who not only cut off his son's allowance, but also refused to accept Camille as one of the family.

Rejection of the Everyday

Monet's success at the Salon gave him some relief from his financial difficulties. In the summer of 1866, he painted another large canvas, 8 feet, 4 inches (2.54 m) by 6 feet, 7 inches (2 m). Intended for the 1867 Salon, *Femmes au Jardin*, or *Women in the Garden*, depicts four women in expensive dresses, three of them posed by Camille. Monet had to rent the garments since he could not afford to buy them. Like *Luncheon on the Grass*, the painting shows the women in natural poses: one smelling a bouquet, another picking flowers, and a third woman holding flowers on her lap. This picture was one of the largest ever created *en plein air*, and the canvas was so big that Monet had to dig a trench in the garden and

lower the painting into it with cables and pulleys so he could work on the upper area.

Much to the artist's dismay, *Women in the Garden* was rejected by the conservative judges on the Salon jury. In her book *Monet*, Vanessa Potts described why they did not think it was worthy of exhibition:

> *Monet was aiming to make two significant points with [this painting]. This large size of canvas was traditionally reserved for historical or religious paintings that carried a moral message for the viewer. By painting an unremarkable modern scene, Monet was declaring that these everyday moments, painted in a realistic manner, were just as important in the art world as esteemed historical or religious subjects. His second point was concerned with the spontaneity of art, and painting exactly what was in front of the artist. Instead of sketching the scene and then completing it in the studio, Monet painted the entire work in the open air.*[14]

The Salon jury also disapproved of the manner in which Monet painted the leaves and foliage in the painting, using dots and patches of color rather than blending the colors together to create realistic detail. Monet further explored this type of stylized painting, which would later become the

The Salon rejected Women in the Garden, *a large painting that elevated an ordinary scene to the level of a historic masterpiece.*

hallmark of Impressionism, in his next work, *Jeanne-Marguerite Lecadre in the Garden.*

Success and a Double Life

Although the Salon rejected *Women in the Garden*, the influential novelist Émile Zola believed the painting was Monet's greatest so far. Zola called Monet and other artists such as Bazille *Les Actualistes.* The name meant that its members were actual or authentic. According to Zola, these were people whose "works are alive because they have taken them from life and they have painted them with all the love they feel for modern subjects."[15]

Zola's words appeared in a Salon review published in *L'Événement,* a major Paris newspaper. Around this time, Bazille helped Monet out of debt by buying *Women in the Garden* for the stunning amount of 2,500 francs, an amount equal to the annual salary of a French factory worker at the time. Unfortunately, Monet could not feel the satisfaction of instant wealth because Bazille agreed to pay the artist only 50 francs a month for 50 months. Oftentimes, the money was not paid in a timely manner, and Monet was forced to write dozens of letters to Bazille pleading poverty and begging for his money. A typical letter reads, "I'm really angry with you; I didn't think you would abandon me like this, it really is too bad. It's now almost a month since I asked you first [for my monthly payment]: since then ... I've waited for the postman every day and it's the same. For the last time I'm asking you for this *favor.*"[16]

At the time of the letter, Camille was in Paris, pregnant with Monet's child, but the impoverished artist was living at his aunt's house in Sainte-Adresse. Monet left Paris not only to save money but to beg his father to accept Camille and their child. Although Monet's father had recently fathered a child with his own mistress, he refused his son's request and coldly instructed Monet to abandon Camille if he expected financial support from the family. Meanwhile, Monet remained in Sainte-Adresse, leaving Camille with no food and no blanket, crib, or toys for his son Jean Armand Claude, who was born August 8, 1867. After the birth, Monet lied to his father, saying the relationship was over, but the artist spent the next seven months shuttling back and forth between Camille's small Paris apartment and Sainte-Adresse. Monet would disappear for short periods only so his father would not suspect his defiance.

Monet's art did not suffer while he was living this double life. Between the summer of 1867 and March 1868, the artist completed more than 20 medium-size canvases along with 2 large paintings for entry into the Salon exhibition. Of the large paintings, *The Luncheon,* which was an

In 1868, the Salon rejected The Luncheon because again, Monet emphasized what was considered to be unimportant family life on a large scale.

indoor scene with four figures in odd, spontaneous poses, was rejected. Again Monet depicted an ordinary family scene—Camille and baby Jean enjoying a meal—on a large scale normally reserved for historical events. As the Städel Museum in Germany, which now houses the painting, noted,

> The composition likewise contradicted every tradition. For example, the painter emphasized such matters of minor importance as the food on the table; indeed, he integrated an entire still life. He emphasized the emotional focus—his little boy— by casting the brightest light on him and on his mother; at the same time, however, he pushed the child to the far edge of the scene. What is more, the right hand edge of the canvas cuts harshly through the table and chair.[17]

Hard Times in Bonnières-sur-Seine

Soon after the 1868 Salon exhibition, Monet returned to the Le Havre region to paint pier and shipping scenes for another important art show, the International Maritime Exhibition to be held in Le Havre in July 1868. In order to concentrate on his work, he moved with Camille and his son to an inn located in the small town of Bonnières-sur-Seine, about 40 miles (65 km) northwest of Paris. Although Monet's living conditions at the cheap rooming house were dirty and unpleasant, the inn was located in a remote spot, accessible only by an aged ferryboat. The countryside around the inn was beautiful, surrounded by green meadows, wildflowers, and butterflies.

In this pastoral, or peaceful country, setting, Monet painted *The River*, depicting Camille sitting on a riverbank staring out over the water. According to French art critic and artist biographer Jean-Paul Crespelle in *Monet*, this is "probably the first painting that is totally Impressionist in spirit. All the elements are there: water, iridescence, reflections, pale colors, colored shadows and, above all, that atmosphere of euphoria that is the movement's hallmark."[18]

The euphoria in the painting stood in sharp contrast to Monet's real life. Unable to pay the bills at the inn, he was evicted after a few months. Monet had to find temporary shelter for Camille and his infant son while he went to Paris in a desperate effort to borrow money from creditors. In a letter to Bazille, Monet talked about a suicide attempt:

> I must have been born under an unlucky star. I've just been turned out, without even a shirt to my back, from the inn where I was staying ... [My] family refuses to do anything more for me and

I don't even know yet where I'll be sleeping tomorrow ... I was so upset yesterday that I was stupid enough to hurl myself into the water [of the Seine River]. Fortunately no harm was done.[19]

Monet's mood improved considerably when five of his paintings were included in the Maritime Exhibition. One of them, a painting of the port of Le Havre that had been rejected by the Salon earlier in the year, won a silver medal.

Coastal Living

In October 1868, Monet moved his family to Étretat, a village on the Normandy coast. He seemed to find happiness in Étretat. Writing to Bazille, Monet stated,

I'm surrounded here by all that I love. I spend my time out-of-doors on the [beach] when the weather's stormy or when the boats go out fishing; otherwise I go into the country, which is so lovely here that I perhaps find it even more agreeable in the winter than in summer; and naturally I'm working all the time, and I think this year I'm going to do some serious things ... I am enjoying the most perfect tranquility and ... would like to stay this way forever in a peaceful corner of the countryside.[20]

Like so many other times in Monet's life, trouble quickly followed success. In late 1868, when the Maritime Exhibition closed, the artist's creditors seized his unsold paintings and auctioned them off to the highest bidder. Fortunately, Louis-Joachim Gaudibert, a wealthy collector in Le Havre, was able to purchase the paintings and return them to the artist. Nevertheless, the incident caused Monet much anguish, causing him to destroy several paintings to keep them out of the hands of his creditors.

Monet's spirits brightened temporarily when he began planning his next submissions for the Salon in early 1869. He began work on a seascape, *Fishing Boats at Sea*. The artist also decided to submit a winter landscape, *The Magpie, Snow Effect, Outskirts of Honfleur*, painted in the countryside near Étretat.

The Magpie Disappointment

Painted on a frigid late afternoon in the middle of winter, *The Magpie, Snow Effect, Outskirts of Honfleur* depicts a snow-covered wicker fence, woven from tree branches. A tan barn sits in the background shrouded by snow-laden trees, while the blue and purple shadows of late afternoon give the scene a forlorn feeling. A lone magpie perches on a small ladder on the left side of the canvas. Like most of Monet's subjects at the time, the bird is facing away from the viewer. It is the only other creature—besides the painter—out on such a desolate afternoon, and like the painter, the magpie seems to be pondering the light of the distant sea reflected on the vast horizon.

In *Monet: His Life and Complete Works*, Sophie Monneret calls *The Magpie, Snow Effect, Outskirts of Honfleur*, "one of Monet's absolute masterpieces."[21] The Salon disagreed, however, and rejected the painting along with *Fishing Boats at Sea*. Monet felt this snub was a disaster. In a letter to French novelist Arsène Houssaye, he wrote, "After this failure I can no longer claim to cope … [That] fatal rejection has virtually taken the bread out of my mouth, and despite my extremely modest prices, dealers and art lovers are turning their backs on me. It is, above all, very depressing to see the lack of interest shown in an art object which has no market value."[22] Monet's self-pity was also tinged with jealousy. Paintings by Manet, Renoir, Degas, Pissarro, and Bazille had all been accepted by the Salon.

A bright spot during this period came from gallery owner Louis Latouche,

The Beach at Trouville

In the summer of 1870, Monet spent an extended vacation in the fashionable resort town of Trouville with his family, friend, and mentor Eugène Boudin and Boudin's wife. Over the years, Boudin had successfully marketed paintings of the resort, and Monet thought he might take advantage of the public's enthusiasm for canvases of the vacation spot. However, as often before, Monet refused to make commercial paintings and instead pursued his own distinctive style. In *Monet*, Vanessa Potts explained the singularity of the work *The Beach at Trouville*:

> [This] picture depicts both Camille and Boudin's wife on the beach … Monet's choice of subject again reflects his desire to record modern scenes. He chose to show this familiar resort in an untraditional way. Firstly the viewer is thrust in very close to the two women … The result is to make the viewer slightly uncomfortable, as if he were invading an intimate scene. This discomfort is furthered by the relationship between the two women. The central space between them is empty; neither woman acknowledges the presence of the other. Their features are not detailed so there is an air of anonymity about them … In the background other tourists can be seen, also devoid of identifiable features. This, combined with the quick, heavy brushstrokes, adds to the spontaneity of the painting.[1]

Monet painted Camille and Eugène Boudin's wife using heavy brushstrokes.

1. Vanessa Potts, *Monet*. Bath, UK: Parragon, 2001, p. 50.

Monet was desolate after the Salon rejected
The Magpie, Snow Effect, Outskirts of Honfleur.

who was intrigued by Monet's evolving style. When Latouche placed one of the artist's scenes from Sainte-Adresse in the window of his Paris gallery, the work attracted large crowds who excitedly discussed the new style of painting. This did little to help Monet's financial situation, however.

Early Signs of Impressionism

Monet realized he needed to be closer to Paris to survive as an artist. In the spring of 1869, with funds borrowed from Gaudibert, Monet and his family moved to a small cottage in the rural community of Saint-Michel in the hills above a popular Seine resort west of Paris. Now Monet could easily travel by train to Paris, but his attempts to sell his paintings failed. Within months, the artist's finances hit rock bottom. His friend Renoir, who was living with his parents in a nearby vil

Going to the Extreme

Monet was fascinated with the way the winter light reflected off the snow and ice in the French countryside. Some of his greatest masterpieces, such as *The Magpie, Snow Effect, Outskirts of Honfleur*, were painted outdoors when temperatures plunged below zero. When art critic Léon Billot discovered Monet working in a frigid field, he described the scene for the newspaper *Journal du Havre*:

> It was during winter, after several snowy days ... The desire to see the countryside beneath its white shroud had led us across the fields. It was cold enough to split rocks. We glimpsed a little heater, then an easel, then a gentleman, swathed in three overcoats, with gloved hands, his face half-frozen. It was [Monsieur] Monet, studying an aspect of the snow. We must confess that this pleased us. Art has some courageous soldiers.[1]

1. Léon Billot, "Fine Arts Exhibition" in *Monet: A Retrospective*, ed. Charles F. Stuckey. New York, NY: Park Lane, p. 40.

lage, helped Monet by raiding his family's pantry to provide food for Camille and her baby. Even with this help, Renoir told Bazille, "At Monet's house ... things are getting serious. They don't eat every day."[23]

History has shown, however, that Monet often exaggerated his poverty to extract funds from his benefactors. Additionally, despite Renoir's comments, Monet wrote to Bazille around the same time and asked for a cask of wine and for the cost to be deducted from the money Bazille owed him.

Another hint that things were not as bad as they seemed may be seen in the artist's work during this period. From the time he arrived in Saint-Michel to the time he left for Paris a year later, Monet produced about 20 canvases that can only be described as joyful and peaceful. Several of them were created at the boating and swimming resort at nearby La Grenouillère. Sitting side by side, Renoir and Monet refined the language of Impressionism. Monet's *La Grenouillère* captures a moment in time, a quick glance at boats, bathers, well-dressed tourists, rippling waters, and a café on the Seine.

La Grenouillère *was an early example of Impressionism.*

Today, *La Grenouillère* is considered a classic example of early Impressionism, and the place where it was painted is permanently linked to Monet and Renoir. However, Monet submitted a similar painting he made at La Grenouillère to the Salon jury of 1870, and it was rejected.

While Monet was pioneering a new painting style, the rejection by the Salon was still painful. Canvases by Renoir, Bazille, and Pissarro had been accepted along with about 3,000 other works—3 times more than were shown in the Salon of 1865. Monet may have found it somewhat encouraging that his rejection caused uproar in the art world and the decision to reject was not unanimous. Two of the judges quit in protest, and the issue was covered in the press when Houssaye wrote an article in the widely read magazine *L'Artiste* in which he praised Monet.

Camille was a frequent subject of Monet's paintings, such as **Camille on the Beach in Trouville**, *shown here. This painting was created on their honeymoon in 1870.*

Newlyweds on the Normandy Coast

Five years after they met, Monet and Camille decided to marry in June 1870. They had already been living together for about four years and had a nearly three-year-old son. Suspicious that Monet married his daughter for her dowry (the transfer of money or property from a bride to a husband upon marriage), Charles-Claude Doncieux gave his daughter only 10 percent of her anticipated dowry, 1,200 francs, with the remaining 10,000-plus francs to be paid after the elder Doncieux died. Camille's parents required that her personal money be kept in an account under her name to protect it from Monet's creditors.

The Monets used the money they did receive from Camille's father to take a honeymoon trip to Trouville, a beautiful town on the Normandy coast, not far from Le Havre across the mouth of the Seine River. Mary Mathews Gedo theorized in her book *Monet and His Muse: Camille Monet in the Artist's Life* that perhaps Monet traveled to the coast in the hopes that his marriage to Camille would reconcile him with his father and Aunt Lecadre. He would never introduce his new wife to his aunt, though, as Sophie Lecadre died within days of his marriage.

The newlyweds spent several weeks in Trouville, staying at the Hôtel Tivoli where they wracked up a sizeable bill that would eventually go unpaid. Monet completed 11 paintings during this time, either of Camille along the beach or landscapes of the boardwalk, shops, and hotel, such as *The Hôtel des Roches-Noires, Trouville*.

It is likely Monet was able to mend the issues with his father during a visit to Le Havre in September 1870. After that visit, Monet, his wife, and his son were able to move to London, England, and rent an elegant residence, possibly using funds from Monet's father.

CHAPTER THREE

Argenteuil and Retreat from War

Nearly a month after Monet's marriage to Camille, while the two were still honeymooning in Trouville, France declared war on Prussia. This launched the Franco-Prussian War, a conflict lasting from July 1870 to May 1871 that was fought over expanding German unification under the Prussian king. As he painted tourists and happy beach scenes, Monet avoided conscription (forced enlistment in the military), though some of his artist friends were not as lucky. Renoir was enlisted into the cavalry, Bazille joined the army, and Degas and Manet volunteered for the National Guard.

Though catastrophe was closing in—the Prussian army had surrounded Paris by September—Monet's paintings reflected little of the threat of the war. The only hint of national upheaval in his Trouville paintings are French flags hanging in front of the beachfront hotels, though "the artist was no doubt accurately depicting the actual scene in these instances,"[24] writer Mary Mathews Gedo stated. However, Monet could not remain immune to the tragedies of war, and in late 1870, he learned Bazille—a good friend and a dependable source of funding—had been killed in battle. Facing the threat of being enlisted into the military, Monet visited Le Havre to obtain a passport before meeting up with Camille and Jean in London.

The only hint of the ongoing Franco-Prussian War in Monet's work at this time was the presence of French flags outside the hotels in Trouville, shown here in The Hôtel des Roches-Noires, Trouville, *painted in 1870.*

Painting the Gloom of London

By the time Monet arrived in London, the city was filling with French exiles, many of them artists or wealthy patrons of the arts. Among them was painter Charles-François Daubigny, an old friend of Monet's who introduced the artist to exiled art dealer Paul Durand-Ruel. Paul Hayes Tucker described the historic significance of this event:

> [This] trip provided [Monet] with an economic windfall as Daubigny ... insisted that Durand-Ruel purchase works from this up-and-coming artist. It was probably the most important introduction Monet ever received as Durand-Ruel soon became Monet's main conduit for selling pictures and his primary source of funds for more than three decades.[25]

Initially, Durand-Ruel purchased only one painting, *Breakwater at Trouville, Low Tide*, and he chose to display the canvas at the opening of his new art gallery on London's fashionable Bond Street. Called the Annual Exhibitions of the Society of French Artists, this show was the first of 10 annual events that displayed the work of French painters to a British audience.

Just as Londoners were learning about French art, Monet was able for the first time to study British painters firsthand. London's celebrated National Gallery exhibited dozens of works by renowned artists John Constable and J. M. W. Turner, neither of whom was shown in Paris. Monet was particularly inspired by Turner's seascapes and landscapes and the way in which the English artist painted the effects of light. As John Piper wrote in *British Romantic Artists*, Turner "painted *light*— veiled light, or misty light, or full light, or blinding light."[26]

Doubtlessly, Turner's paintings such as the *Lausanne* series, with their shimmering colors, intense contrasts, and barely recognizable subjects, were closely studied by Monet. Of the six canvases Monet later painted in London, two scenes of the Thames River show the influence of the *Lausanne* paintings. Unlike his bright, cheery canvases of the Normandy coast, however, *The Thames Below Westminster* and *Boats in the Port of London* show the typical gloomy weather of the British winter. These gray canvases may have suited the artist's mood since they were created around the time Monet's father died in Sainte-Adresse. While saddened by the death, Monet was also disappointed to learn that his father had left him only a very small inheritance, which he would receive the following year.

The Thames Below Westminster *illustrates the gloom of a typical British winter and reflects Monet's exposure to British artists such as J. M. W. Turner and John Constable.*

Summer in Holland

By the time Monet left London in May 1871, the Franco-Prussian War had ended. France lost the war, but the peace settlement stipulated that the Prussians were to leave Paris. Even so, the city remained in turmoil. An attempt by a large group of Socialists called the Paris Commune to seize control of the government was brutally repressed by the French military.

Although the war was over, Monet was still fearful of returning to Paris. Instead, he went to Holland, using money from the first purchase of his paintings by Durand-Ruel. After traveling by train through the country, he settled in early June in the small village of Zaandam, just outside of Amsterdam. Holland, with its ancient windmills, large tulip gardens, pleasant countryside, and beautiful canals,

Monet created Windmill at Zaandam, *shown here, after being inspired by the windmills.*

strongly appealed to Monet.

The artist also appreciated the Dutch people, many of whom spoke perfect French and respected artists whether or not they were famous. Writing to Pissarro about his experiences, Monet stated that Holland "is much more beautiful than what they say … [and Zaandam has] houses of all colors, windmills by the hundreds, and enchanting boats … There is enough to paint here for a lifetime."[27] During the summer in Holland, Monet produced 24 paintings, including *The Port of Zaandam*, *The Zaan River at Zaandam*, and *Windmill at Zaandam*. He also had his photograph taken by Albert Greiner, a German photographer working in Amsterdam. The picture shows a thoughtful Monet with his longish beard, peering somewhat suspiciously at the camera.

New Inspiration in Argenteuil

Monet returned to Paris in the autumn

of 1871. Many important public buildings, including the Tuileries Palace, the Palais-Royal, and the Palais de Justice, lay in ruins. Typically, Monet's paintings did not reveal a hint of the destruction of his city nor the hardships suffered by his friends who witnessed mass famine and death. In fact, despite the depressing situation in Paris, Monet was beginning to enjoy the most successful years of his career thus far. Durand-Ruel was buying his paintings on a regular basis, and the dealer had gathered a large base of wealthy customers who were interested in Monet's style.

In December 1871, Monet moved his family to a rented house in Argenteuil with a view of the Seine. The move to this scenic countryside town, which was then home to about 8,000 people, gave Monet easy access to Paris, just a few miles to the south.

Argenteuil also attracted other painters including Manet, Boudin, Sisley, and Renoir. The wealth of artistic scenery, both pastoral and modern, is described by Tucker in *The Impressionists at Argenteuil*:

> *Argenteuil's appeal to the impressionists derived mostly from its diversity, which offered something for everyone. Depending on where one looked, the town could be charmingly historic or unnervingly progressive. Monet encountered these contrasts on a daily basis. Directly across the street from his house on the rue Pierre Guienne ... stood an impressive eighteenth-century building that served as the town hospice. When he walked out his front door, he could see the newly renovated Boulevard Héloïse ... and the promenade to the right. If he turned to his left, he could see the railroad station and several factories, beyond which stretched residential streets that led to the vineyards and the Orgemont hill with its windmill restaurant. Everything was within walking distance.* [28]

For the first time, Monet was able to live in the grand style he had desired for so long. He entertained other artists at his home and purchased a substantial quantity of wine to share with his guests. He hired two domestic servants and a gardener.

France Emerges from Disaster

During Monet's first year at Argenteuil, he produced 60 paintings. Several, such as and *Jean Monet on His Hobby Horse*, included the artist's wife and son as subjects. Monet also created many paintings of everyday scenes around Argenteuil. These include *Houses at the Edge of the Field*, showing new housing developments, and *Spring in Argenteuil*, a pastoral riverbank scene nearly untouched by humanity. Monet depicts the leisurely pace of life along the river with

Living in Style in Argenteuil

By early 1872, Monet's paintings were finally selling, and this provided him with enough money to move his family to an idyllic home in Argenteuil. The artist's life at the time is described by Sue Rose in *The Private Lives of the Impressionists*:

Fellow Impressionist painter Manet was so amused by Monet's studio boat, he immortalized his friend and Camille in The Boat (Claude Monet in His Floating Studio).

---

1. Sue Rose, *The Private Lives of the Impressionists*. New York, NY: HarperCollins, 2006, p. 100.

Monet's house was spacious, with parquet floors, French windows, and a ravishing country garden teeming with color in summer. He could stand on his lawn and watch the boats coming and going [on the Seine], and all the activity of the riverside. On sunny days, a table was spread with a glistening white cloth beneath the large horse-chestnut tree, and the family lunched out of doors, little Jean playing on the grass. Monet painted the scene, with Camille's hat hanging in the bough of the chestnut tree, its ribbon trailing from the branches ...

The spring of 1872 was fresh and radiant. Gardens and orchards seemed to bloom all at once ... Suddenly, there was enough money to buy a small boat ... Monet had a wooden cabin built on it and set it up as a small studio, just big enough to take his easel. Manet painted [Monet] in his studio boat, knees drawn up, hat brim turned down, floating on the river, absorbed in painting the water. Inside the house, Monet painted Camille through the French windows, framed by the open russet-colored shutters festooned with flowers. She wore pale pink and blue dresses that summer, with little white collars and pretty hats all decorated with flowers. In some paintings, posed against the banks of flowers, she seems to rise up from a haze of pulsating color.[1]

stunning colors, dreamy cloud-filled skies, transitory shadows, and light that almost shimmers upon the canvas in *The Promenade at Argenteuil, The Basin at Argenteuil,* and *Pleasure Boats at Argenteuil.* These paintings featured typical subject matter for Monet.

In addition to everyday scenes around Argenteuil, Monet also painted scenes that showed the changes that war and industrialization had brought to Argenteuil. For example, *The Highway Bridge Under Repair* shows the city's main bridge over the Seine that had been blown up during the war. Unlike the beautiful subjects often chosen by Monet, this painting is dull, utilizing browns, grays, olive greens, and muted blues to depict a sad mood. The dreary bridge is reflected in the water as the smoke from a factory rises into the distant sky. On top of the bridge, a horse-drawn carriage and a dozen silhouetted figures make their way along the span. Describing the painting, Tucker observed:

This is not a place of reverie or retreat; it does not even fall into the category of the obviously "beautiful."

Monet painted the everyday activities his family did, as seen in paintings such as Jean Monet on His Hobby Horse, *shown here.*

Instead, this is the work-a-day world of daily jobs and commuting and anonymous encounters in repetitive situations. Tentative but determined, loosely painted but highly calculated, the scene suggests that some of the [tensions] of modern life are present even in those areas outside the city which many urban dwellers hoped were free of such strains. These tensions—between labor and leisure, familiarity and aloofness, the human and the natural—were particularly poignant [meaningful] for a nation emerging from the disasters of the previous year.[29]

Nineteenth-century art collectors viewed such paintings as proof that France was reemerging as a strong nation after the crushing defeat by the Prussians.

Solidifying a Movement

Monet's most iconic canvas of the era was not painted in Argenteuil. It was painted in the artist's hometown of Le Havre. Monet had created several sketches and paintings of Le Havre's inner harbor looking out the window of his room at the Hôtel de l'Amirauté at different times of the day.

The painting *Impression, Sunrise* captures the harbor at a fleeting instant when the sun emerged from the mist, silhouetting vague shapes of ship masts and buildings in the distance. Although most of the canvas is painted in subdued, or soft and dim, tones of bluish-lavender, green, and gray, the bright orange fire of the sun leaves a streak on the surface of the water and adds tones of pink, orange, and red to the dawn sky.

Impression, Sunrise was one of

While artists had already been using the term Impressionism to describe their style, the movement was solidified with Monet's creation of Impression, Sunrise.

Common Subjects

Monet and his friends, who were all Impressionist painters, worked together regularly at Argenteuil, oftentimes rendering, or recreating, the same subjects. Tucker explained in *The Impressionists at Argenteuil*:

> [It] might have been possible to mistake a canvas by Monet for one by Renoir ... at Argenteuil. Time and again in the 1870s Monet stood side by side with one of his artist friends rendering the same scene: The Boulevard Héloïse, a

Monet and his friends often put the same subjects to canvas at Argenteuil and they also painted and drew each other, as in Monet's Manet Painting in Monet's Garden in Argenteuil.

1. Paul Hayes Tucker, *The Impressionists at Argenteuil*. Washington, DC: National Gallery of Art, 2000, p. 23.

regatta on the Seine, the boat basin with sailboats and [oars], the railroad bridge ... Sisley was first to join Monet in Argenteuil, and they initiated the custom. Monet and Renoir, the second to visit, soon followed suit. Manet worked beside Renoir once, both of them painting Monet's wife Camille and son Jean in Monet's backyard.

The impressionists also produced many pictures of each other during their stays with Monet. Renoir sketched or painted his host four times and Camille as many; Manet did two portraits of Monet painting in his studio boat with Camille by his side as well as one of the whole family; Monet painted at least one image of Manet in the garden. This habit not only deepened their friendships and avoided the expense of models, it encouraged them to support one another in the face of the challenges they had so ambitiously posed for themselves. In the process, they were able to fulfill their equally important aim to base art on life, and, as an added benefit, they could elevate themselves and their practice to a level of significance that affirmed their claims to history.[1]

many canvases the artist was creating every month. Around this time, Monet had produced enough such paintings to sell another 26 to Durand-Ruel for 12,100 francs in 1872. Pictures of Durand-Ruel's collection of Monet's paintings were published in the art dealer's voluminous catalog, and the preface to the edition was written by respected art critic Armand Silvestre. The critic pointed out for the first time that works by Monet, Sisley, and Pissarro were similar in style and that this group of artists was different from other contemporary painters because their harmonious approach was making a fresh impact on viewers. Silvestre stated that of this group, Monet was the most daring painter of his generation.

Influence of Japanese Art

Another observation stood out in Silvestre's preface. He noted that Monet's irregular brushstrokes were similar to those seen in Japanese images hand-printed from blocks of wood. Doubtlessly, Monet was influenced by Japanese prints. The artist had first seen such prints on wrapping

Japanese artists such as Katsushika Hokusai often painted in flat plains of color with horizons high in the composition, unlike most Western art standards.

paper in an Amsterdam food shop in 1871, and he was so taken with their beauty, he bought a Japanese engraving that was hanging on the wall. He went on to collect 231 of the prints.

Prints by 19th-century Japanese masters such as Katsushika Hokusai and Kitagawa Utamaro were extremely popular in Paris at that time. They featured flattened or tilted spaces, vibrant colors, no shadows, and unbalanced or asymmetrical compositions that did not follow traditional Western art standards. The Japanese artists emphasized small gestures in subjects or casual details and also had a profound reverence for nature. In discussing the influence of Japanese art on Monet, journalist Don Morrison wrote in *TIME* magazine: "Printmaking is a more cumbersome and less forgiving process than painting, so Japanese artists developed a

Japanese Art and the Impressionists

Monet was fascinated by Japanese art prints that became popular in France in the 1870s and 1880s. He collected 231 Japanese art prints, and these works came to be extremely influential among Impressionist painters. The prints depicted landscapes such as Mount Fuji, historical tales, and battle scenes. They also focused on the urban culture of Tokyo. Hand-printed with wooden blocks, the inexpensive prints were known as ukiyo-e, or "images of the floating world." This phrase refers to the youth culture of Tokyo, so-called because the youth were thought to be a society unto themselves, lost in their own floating world.

French artists such as Monet, Manet, and Pissarro became fascinated with ukiyo-e and other products of Japanese culture. This was part of a fad among artists and intellectuals called Japonisme, or love of the Japanese style. It was a result of Japan opening its long-isolated society to outsiders in the 1870s. As trade barriers fell, European department stores and art galleries were suddenly filled with ukiyo-e.

Monet never traveled to Japan. However, because of his artistic eye, he only purchased the highest-quality prints created by masters such as Utagawa Hiroshige, Katsushika Hokusai, and Kitagawa Utamaro.

remarkable economy of expression. Utamaro, for instance, could with a mere line or two describe the course of a river ... Thus could Monet—in Impression, Sunrise ... conjure up a boat with a mere squiggle of the brush."[30]

Rejecting the Salon

While Silvestre praised Monet's Japanese influences, the jurors at the Salon were less impressed. In 1873, fearing another rejection, Monet decided to shun the Salon and hold his own show with other Impressionists. This exhibition of independent artists was the first show held in Paris without government, commercial, or private financial support. The artists would sponsor themselves. After a series of meetings at Argenteuil with Pissarro, Degas, Renoir, Sisley, and others, the artists banded together to form the Anonymous Society of Painters, Sculptors, Printmakers, etc.

The first Impressionist exhibition opened on April 15, 1874, in a gallery on the Boulevard des Capucines, the center of the Paris art world. The exhibit included 160 paintings representing 29 artists. Monet displayed nine paintings, including Impression, Sunrise. During the one-month exhibit, the show received extensive coverage in Paris newspapers and was attended by about 3,500 people. At least 50 art critics reviewed the show. Most reviews were favorable, and Jules Castagnary, writing in *Le Siècle*, described the term "Impressionist" for the first time in print:

> The consensus that unites [these painters] and makes them a collective force in our disintegrated age, is their determination not to seek an exact rendition but to stop at a general appearance. Once that impression is fixed, they declare that their part is played ... If we must characterize them with one explanatory word, we would have to coin a new term: Impressionists. They are Impressionists in that they render not the landscape but the sensation evoked by the landscape. The very word has entered their language: not landscape but impressionism, in the title given in the catalog for Monet's [Impression,] Sunrise. From this point of view, they have left reality behind for a realm of pure idealism. [31]

Several other reviews of the show were scathing. Writing in *La Presse*, Emile Cardon stated: "The scribblings of a child have a naiveté and sincerity that make you smile; the debaucheries [excessive indulgence] of this school are nauseating and revolting."[32] The most famous review of the show, however, was a satire written by landscape artist Louis Leroy. His widely read lampoon (public criticism) in *Le Charivari* was responsible for popularizing the term "Impressionism." In the piece, Leroy imagined the dialogue of an old-fashioned painter, Vincent, upon viewing *Impression, Sunrise*: "This one is Papa Vincent's favorite! ... *Impression Sunrise. Impression*—I knew it. I was just saying to myself, if I'm impressed, there must be an impression in there ... Wallpaper in its embryonic [beginning] state is more labored than this seascape."[33]

The Anonymous Society of Painters, Sculptors, Printmakers, etc. did not use the term "Impressionism" until their third art show in 1877, which was called Exhibition of Impressionists. This was the only time the expression was officially used by the painters. It is likely that they did not want to be limited by the label.

A Productive Period

Monet's output of Impressionist painting continued at an amazing pace. Throughout the mid-1870s the artist continued to paint Argenteuil and the surrounding area including railroad and highway bridges, the view from his backyard, the promenade along the Seine, views from his studio boat, and summer regattas. While the subjects were similar, each painting was different, influenced by the clouds and shadows, the angle of the sun, the time of day, and the various seasons. Drawing on these inspirations, Monet

The influence of Japanese art on Monet manifested itself in 1876 in the painting Camille Monet in Japanese Costume.

Argenteuil and Retreat from War **55**

produced 40 canvases in the summer of 1874 alone.

Monet also continued to paint Camille and Jean in various poses, several of which are timeless classics that define the era. *Woman with a Parasol—Madame Monet and Her Son* was hung at the second impressionist exhibition in 1876. As Monneret wrote,

> *Camille is standing at the top of the hill which her son has not yet reached ... The small, hard, fast, stabbing touches [of Monet's brush] give the foreground of the meadow a kind of motion accentuated by the range of greens barely tinged by the yellow of a few small indecisive flowers. Longer touches swirl the clouds, which the wind seems to be shredding. It shakes [Camille's] sun shade, sweeps up the skirt, blows back the veil. Monet receives those visual sensations and transmits them to the viewer.*[34]

Another painting of Camille, *La Japonaise (Camille Monet in Japanese Costume)*, clearly illustrates Monet's fascination with Japanese art. Camille poses in a long, red kimono, with an uncharacteristic smile, holding a Japanese fan to her face. Monet produced *La Japonaise* for the second impressionist exhibition to show he could paint something other than landscapes. The painting was the intense focus of Paris art critics. Many compared it positively to *Camille (The Woman in the Green Dress)*, Monet's triumph from the 1866 Salon. It is probable the artist was hoping for the same type of payoff from the new painting.

The Monets and the Hoschedés

By 1877, Monet struggled with a number of problems that would cause him to move yet again. An economic downturn in France impacted his own personal finances when his main source of income, Durand-Ruel, stopped buying canvases. Monet once again faced angry creditors and asked friends and colleagues for loans to help pay the butcher or buy supplies. Additionally, Argenteuil no longer provided the historic, charming setting with which he first fell in love. Industry in the small town grew rapidly around this time with the creation of an iron foundry, a distillery, a chemical plant, and a new railroad line—all of which produced clouds of air pollution. The construction of a new sewer line pushed stinking raw sewage into the Seine and the boat basin where Monet kept his studio boat. For a painter who thrived on unspoiled, clean light and natural beauty, it simply would not do.

Disappointed by the town where he entertained fellow artists, explored an interest in Japanese art, and created dozens of the first paintings known for his trademark Impressionist style, Monet wanted to move his family yet again. This time they headed to Vétheuil, a smaller town northwest of Argenteuil. In 1878, Monet, Camille, their newborn son Michel, and Jean took in the family of Ernest Hoschedé, one of Monet's art patrons who had recently filed for bankruptcy. Thus began an intense interest in the painter.

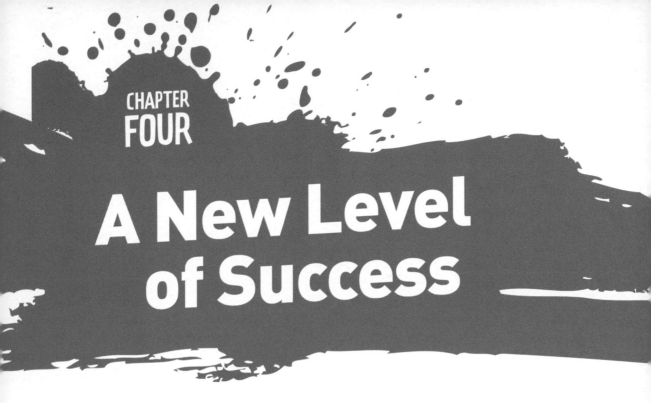

CHAPTER FOUR

A New Level of Success

In Vétheuil, Monet was removed from the city life of Paris and the industrial expansion of Argenteuil, but his life was yet again about to undergo an upheaval. Camille became sick shortly after giving birth to her second child with Monet. In March 1878, Monet wrote to art collector and physician Georges de Bellio that he was in despair over both his wife's illness and his own struggles for success. When Camille's situation became more serious in the summer of 1879, Monet wrote again to de Bellio that "the sight of my wife's life in jeopardy … terrifies me, and it is unbearable to see her suffering so much."[35]

Still, Gedo wrote, Camille's illness did not hamper Monet's creative output and he seemed to have left much of her care in the hands of Alice Hoschedé, Ernest Hoschedé's wife and by this time, likely Monet's extramarital romantic interest. Alice wrote to her mother-in-law in August 1879 that "[Madame] Monet's terrible illness takes up all my time, except for the children and piano lessons."[36] Alice believed death would be a great relief of Camille's suffering.

Camille's pain finally came to an end in September 1879 when she was 32. Just prior to Camille's death, Alice, a deeply religious woman, called upon a priest to sanctify the Monets' marriage, which had been conducted in a

Shown here is Camille on Her Deathbed, *which is the last painting of Camille, painted in 1879.*

Camille's Agony

Camille's second pregnancy further weakened her already-sick body. Some modern scholars believe Camille suffered from pelvic cancer. Monet wrote to art collector and physician Georges de Bellio about not only the toll the disease took on Camille, but the toll economic hardship took on himself:

> Her belly and legs are swollen, and often also her face. With all that continuous vomiting and choking, it is enough to make one agonize [with her], especially when one has no strength of one's own left. If, after my description, you have any advice to give, please do so, and it will be followed to the letter. But what I also ask you, dear Monsieur, is to come to our aid with your purse. We are without the least resource. I have some canvases, take them at any price you wish. Please do not remain deaf to our prayers. Send us two or three hundred francs, which would help us out, and with another one hundred francs, I could buy the canvases and colors that I lack for work.[1]

1. Quoted in Mary Mathews Gedo, *Monet and His Muse: Camille Monet in the Artist's Life*. Chicago, IL: University of Chicago Press, p. 200.

civil ceremony. The official recognition of the marriage by the Catholic Church allowed Camille to receive the last sacraments before her death. Alice remarked on this in a letter to her mother-in-law, "Yes, one great happiness for me amongst all this sadness was to see my poor friend receive her God with faith and conviction and receive the last sacraments."[37]

Throughout Camille's illness and during their three years at Vétheuil, Monet was more productive than ever. It was then that he also used Camille as his muse for the final time, immortalizing her in frosty whites, purples, and blues in *Camille on Her Deathbed*.

Winter Landscapes

In the winter of 1879, following Camille's death, France had record-setting cold temperatures that froze the Seine. During this unprecedented weather, Monet braved subzero temperatures to record the freeze and the subsequent thaw in the early months of 1880 on canvas. In paintings such as *Ice Floes on the Seine at Bougival*, *The Frost*, and *Sunset on the Seine at Lavacourt*, Monet recreated scenes of desolate beauty, with bare trees, cold winter light, and massive ice blocks floating down the river. However, as Potts pointed out:

Although the subject matter itself could represent Monet's personal desolation, his treatment of it suggests that this is not the case. The Frost shows ice and frost sparkling in the sunlight, the white frost warmed up with pink and blue. Although a barren scene, the colors used give it a warmth ... The whole scene is harmonized through the use of strong horizontal [brush] strokes on the ice and small vertical strokes on the bushes. The vertical of the poplars balances the horizontal of the river bank.[38]

Whatever Monet's mental state in the winter of 1879, he was not alone with his children. His family shared the large house at Vétheuil with the Hoschedés—Ernest, Alice, their five daughters, and their infant son. Monet had invited the couple to live with him

The winter of 1879 was a particularly harsh one, providing Monet with new, stark landscapes to paint, such as the one shown here in Sunset on the Seine at Lavacourt.

after Ernest lost his huge wealth, his estate, and his art collection during bankruptcy proceedings in 1877. With the two families living together and only Monet's income to support them, little money was left to pay the gardener, maid, and cook, all of whom sued Monet for failure to pay wages. Matters were further complicated when it became apparent that Monet and Alice were involved in a romantic relationship that had been going on for several years. When Ernest discovered this, he moved out of the Vétheuil house.

Hoping to improve his financial situation, Monet entered *Ice Floes on the Seine at Bougival* and *Sunset on the Seine at Lavacourt* in the 1880 Salon. *Sunset on the Seine at Lavacourt* was accepted, but "skyed," or placed so high on the uppermost row of paintings that it could not be easily viewed. Disgusted once again with the Paris art

Guy de Maupassant on Monet

In 1886, French poet and novelist Guy de Maupassant accompanied Monet as he painted the Normandy Coast. During this period, the artist was painting a series of canvases of a single subject. Maupassant wrote the following in an article, "The Life of a Landscapist," for the magazine *Gil Blas*:

> Last year ... I often followed Claude Monet, who was in search of impressions. Actually he was no longer a painter but a hunter [of spontaneous images]. He went along followed by children who carried his canvases, five or six canvases all depicting the same subject at different hours of the day and with different effects. He would take [the canvases] up in turn, then put them down again, depending on the changes in the sky. Standing before his subjects, he waited, watched the sun and the shadows, capturing in a few brushstrokes a falling ray of light or a passing cloud and, scorning false and conventional [painting] techniques, transferred them rapidly onto his canvas. In this way I saw him catch a sparkling stream of light on a white cliff and fix it in a flow of yellow tones that strangely rendered the surprising ... effect of that elusive [difficult to catch] and blinding brilliance. Another time he caught with both hands a torrent [rapidly flowing water] of rain on the sea and flung it on his canvas [in a shower of paint]. It was truly rain that he had thus painted, nothing but rain throwing a veil over the waves, rocks, and sky, which could scarcely be discerned [seen] under this deluge [flood].[1]

1. Guy de Maupassant, "The Life of a Landscapist," in *Monet: A Retrospective*, ed. Charles F. Stuckey. New York, NY: Park Lane, pp. 122–123.

establishment, Monet began to pursue new methods for selling his paintings. His first attempt, a one-artist exhibition held in June 1880, yielded immediate results, and he sold several of his recent canvases. Later, Monet entered his paintings in provincial exhibitions in towns such as Grenoble and Nancy. Although he considered these small art shows beneath his status as a master painter, he was able to meet new collectors through this venture.

The Cliffs of Normandy

Despite his efforts, Monet still did not have enough money to cover his expenses. After conversations about the problem with Durand-Ruel, Monet became convinced that he could make money painting seascapes, which appealed to collectors more than his recent works. The artist had always loved the beauty of the Normandy coast along the English Channel. In early 1881, he made the first of many trips to the region in France to paint stark renderings of the plunging cliffs, desolate beaches, and crashing seas near the villages of Fécamp, Pourville, Varengeville, and Étretat. Over the next five years, Monet traveled extensively to the Normandy coast, filling hundreds of canvases with the magnificent scenery found in the region.

Compared with his views of the Seine completed in Argenteuil and Vétheuil, the Normandy paintings are much more dramatic. The reflection of the light in the ocean, the shades of the foliage, or leaves, on the cliffs, and the impressiveness of the clouds at sunset are all brought to life by Monet's extensive mix of warm colors next to cold colors. These techniques can be seen in *The Cliff at Fécamp*, where dozens of shades of aquamarine green mingle with blue and purple in the sea, contrasting with shades of green, orange, pink, and burgundy along the cliff top. Each brushstroke seems to be of a different color. Single strokes are woven into an intricate pattern, like individual threads on a brightly colored piece of cloth.

The Cliff at Fécamp was one of a series of Grainval paintings created from the same vantage point. In reflecting his philosophy that "landscape is nothing but an impression, and an instantaneous one,"[39] Monet sat and waited for hours watching the sun, waves, and shadows shift. When the moment struck, the artist recorded his impression of the spectacular view in a series of quick brushstrokes. Later, when the light and weather changed, he returned to a small stone house built high above the cliffs to record another scene. The angle from which the artist painted the cliffs from his perch was called a "seagull's view" by Robert L. Herbert in *Monet on the Normandy Coast*. Herbert wrote that "it is an aerial suspension that Monet will exploit repeatedly in coming years."[40]

Monet painted the cliffs at Grainval many times, including The Cliff at Fécamp, *shown here.*

Return to the Coast

The good reviews for Monet's Normandy paintings led to increased interest from art collectors, prompting Monet to return to the coast in February 1882 for two months. Of the 36 paintings created on this trip, 23 of them were promptly purchased by Durand-Ruel, inspiring Monet to return to the English Channel in the summer. This time he took along Alice and the Hoschedés' six children. Paintings such as *Gorge of the Petit Ailly, Fisherman's Cottage on*

Danger on the Cliffs

Monet seemed to thrive on inclement weather and often painted in desolate regions while storms raged around him. In *Monet*, Jean-Jacques Lévêque quoted an anonymous source who watched Monet paint several canvases at the same time on the Normandy Coast:

> [A witness reported having seen] Claude Monet wrapped in a cloak, the rain streaming over him, as he painted in the hurricane, doused by great splashes of salt water. He held two or three canvases between his knees, which at intervals of a few minutes he rotated on the easel. They all framed the same section of a cliff with the raging sea, under different lighting effects, fine infiltrations of light falling through breaks in the clouds ... The painter stalked each of these effects, a slave to the coming and going of light, halting his brush at the close of each of its appearances, setting at his feet the incomplete canvas ... to resume ... another work.[1]

1. Jean-Jacques Lévêque, *Monet*. New York, NY: Crescent, 1990, p. 88.

what he had made in previous years. Clearly, a good market existed for Monet's Impressionist renderings of Normandy. However, as Herbert wrote,

This does not mean Monet thought he was well off ... for he continued to spend more than he earned, and at every stage owed his dealer yet more paintings against advances. He also had a backlog of unpaid bills and was threatened with [legal proceedings] in July for non-payment of a debt of 1,200 francs going back fifteen years; he expected Durand-Ruel to provide the money.[41]

Driven by financial need, Monet continued with his travels in search of inspirational scenery. In early 1883, the artist went to Étretat. There, he created 23 canvases in 3 weeks, painting from the window of his hotel when the weather was too cold to work outdoors. The Étretat region proved to be one of the artist's favorites, and in the following 3 years Monet produced more than 75 paintings there, 50 of them in the cold light of winter or fall.

the *Cliffs at Varengeville*, and *Cliff Walk at Pourville* were among the nearly 90 pictures the artist painted that summer.

Another trip in October yielded more canvases, and all were purchased by Monet's art dealer. This brought his yearly income for 1882 to 31,000 francs, more than 2.5 times

Étretat and the Manneporte Arch

The Étretat paintings differ from Monet's earlier seascapes because of the incredible scenery found in the region. Over the centuries, the coast along this part of the English Channel was carved by wind and water into three dramatic arches that curve out from the cliffs and plunge into the sea. Manneporte, the most spectacular arch, which Monet painted several times, is located next to a pyramid of rock, called the Needle, which juts up out of the water. Tucker described the Manneporte arch: "By its isolation and sheer size, it was both frightening and awe-inspiring, incomprehensible and yet incredibly physical."[42] Above the arches, bright green, lush grass provides a contrast to the sand-colored rock and blue seas below.

Danger as well as beauty lurked beneath the Manneporte arch. To visit the cove below, hikers had to time their walk to coincide with the low tide. When the tide rose, the crashing waves made access to the cove impossible. Over the years, some visitors had been trapped below the arch and swept into the ocean where they drowned. In November 1885, this almost happened to Monet, who, while concentrating on a painting, was thrown against the cliffs by a large wave. The artist, along with his canvas, easel, and paints, was then pulled into the ocean. After a narrow escape, he wrote to Alice, "My immediate thought was that I was done for, as the water dragged me down, but in the end I managed to clamber out on all fours."[43] The canvas, however, was torn to shreds by the waves and rocks, and Monet was angry that he could no longer work until he obtained more art supplies.

Monet put himself in danger because he was seeking new views of Manneporte that had never been put to canvas. This part of France had been painted extensively by Gustave Courbet in the 1870s as well as by dozens of other landscape artists of the early 1800s. This forced Monet to come up with new ways of portraying the cliffs so his canvases would be unique. In pursuit of originality, the artist struggled to find new vantage

Monet's *Étretat paintings, including* The Cliffs at Étretat *(shown here) are known for the incredible scenery in the area.*

points, painting the arches from the beach, from high above in his hotel room, and from close up. He also portrayed them during winter storms, calm seas, with beaches and boats, at sunset, and at high tide (from a safe distance). While painting outdoors in the most extreme conditions, Monet worked in high winds, anchoring his easel with ropes and rocks, wearing heavy winter clothes, or dressing like a fisherman in a hooded oilskin raincoat and rubber boots. However, the artist seemed to thrive in the turbulent weather, writing in the winter of 1886 to Durand-Ruel, "I don't know if the work I bring back will be to everyone's taste ... but what I do know is that this coast enthralls me."[44]

The Lure of Giverny

When Monet first began painting the Normandy coast in 1881, he was living in Vétheuil. In April 1883, however, the artist moved with his extended family to the farming village of Giverny, on the east bank of the Seine where it met with the Epte River. This scenic town 45 miles (74 km) northwest of Paris would be Monet's home until his death in 1926.

Monet rented the largest residence in the town, a pink stucco house on 2.5 acres (1 ha). It was known as *Le Pressoir*, or the Cider Press, for the apple cider made from the estate's orchard. As with his earlier moves, Monet chose Giverny for the artistic possibilities offered by the region, telling Durand-Ruel, "Once settled, I hope to produce masterpieces ... because I like the countryside very much."[45]

Despite the declaration to his art dealer, Monet did not paint in the Giverny region for many years. Immediately after his family moved in, on April 30, 1883, Manet died at the age of 51, and Monet traveled to Paris to attend the funeral. The artist then spent the summer painting on the Normandy coast. Then, at the end of the year, Monet left northern France for the first time since 1870, traveling with Renoir to the Italian Riviera along the coast of the Mediterranean Sea. This was meant to be a painting trip, but Monet felt uncomfortable working with Renoir looking over his shoulder and did not paint. However, Monet appreciated the scenic value of the seaside palm trees, olive trees, and orange groves beneath the bright southern sun.

A Trip to Italy

In early 1884, Monet traveled alone to the Italian village of Bordighera on the Italian Riviera. Describing the artistic possibilities of the region, Monet wrote to Alice:

> It's going to be rather painful for people who can't stand blue and pink, because it's precisely that brilliance, that enchanted light that I'm trying to catch, and anyone who hasn't visited this part of the world will ... believe I've invented it, although actually I'm underplaying the tonal intensity: everything is the blue

of a pigeon's neck or the color of flaming punch.[46]

This beauty, however, overwhelmed the artist, and at times he was fearful that he could not capture it on canvas, telling Durand-Ruel: "It is a magical and terribly difficult land. I would need a palette of diamonds and jewelleries"[47] to recreate the colors.

Despite his insecurities, Monet returned to Giverny with a number of canvases of Italy including *Bordighera* and *Villas at Bordighera*. The painting *Olive Grove in the Moreno Garden* was created in luxurious gardens described by Monet as "pure fairlyand."[48] These gardens, owned by wealthy art patron Francesco Moreno, inspired Monet to plant his own beautiful gardens at Giverny in later years.

Monet was rewarded financially from his work in the Mediterranean. Durand-Ruel bought several of the canvases, which were quickly purchased by collectors. In 1886, Monet became an internationally recognized artist when Durand-Ruel sent 50 of his canvases to New York City for the exhibition "Works in Oil and Pastel by the Impressionists in Paris" at the American Art Gallery. The exhibition of 300 paintings by French artists was extremely popular, and Monet's large contribution garnered widespread critical praise.

The Wild Coast

Fresh off his success in the New York exhibit, Monet traveled to Belle-Île, an island in the Atlantic off the western coast of France. Between September 1886 and December 1886, he painted more than 40 canvases of the harsh, unforgiving landscape of dangerously steep cliffs and large rocky outcrops of the so-called "wild coast." Monet hired a porter to help carry his canvases and other supplies to remote areas of the coast, but the porter quit after two days in the dangerous conditions. The sea was so harsh, gusty winds blew away Monet's supplies, once even taking the brush out of his hand However, the artist was in his element, writing to fellow French painter Gustave Caillebotte, "I am in a wonderfully wild region, with terrifying rocks and a sea of unbelievable colors; I am truly thrilled, even though it is difficult, because I had got used to painting the Channel, and I knew how to go about it, but the Atlantic Ocean is quite different."[49]

However, the canvases he produced on Belle-Île are unlike those he painted on the English Channel coast. Instead of misty seas and hazy clouds, Monet nearly completely eliminates the sky, filling the frame with stark rocks and riotous waves, dashed off, as Potts wrote, "in a frenzy of excitement."[50] The stark landscapes are free of any human intervention, reflecting Monet's 15-year-old interest in Japanese art. The Musée d'Orsay

Storm, off the Coast of Belle-Île, *shows the wild, untamed brushstrokes Monet used on the paintings he created at the location.*

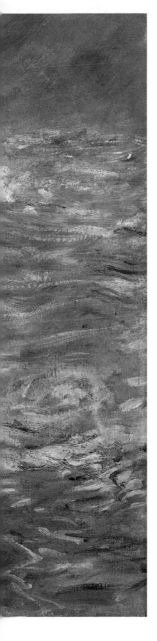

described *The Rocks at Belle-Île, The Wild Coast* on its website:

The rocks are laid out to create a feeling of space. In the style of Japanese prints, which had much in common with Impressionist aesthetics, the horizon is placed at the top of the painting, leaving little room for sky ... Blues, greens and violets run through a sea fringed with white, where the brush strokes are flat and broad, vertical or rounded, like circumflex accents or commas, stormy but controlled. This is a new style of brushwork, very different from Monet's Normandy paintings, and more suited to this awe-inspiring island where everything is beyond Man's control.[51]

Monet's time on Belle-Île was a turning point for the artist. It marked the start of a new painting technique in which he would set up multiple canvases next to each other. He would work on one until the light changed, then would move on to the next, capturing the same landscape with slightly different colors and lighting. He finished the canvases quickly and never returned to them for touch-ups in his studio.

Art critic Gustave Geffroy wrote that Monet captured "the sea, where all is in continuous motion – the shape of the waves, the transparent depths, the variety of foam, the reflections of the sky."[52] However, other artists were less impressed. Fellow Impressionist painter Camille Pissarro said the Belle-Île paintings did "not represent a highly developed art,"[53] while Degas said Monet was less interested in art than in how much money he could make off multiple paintings.

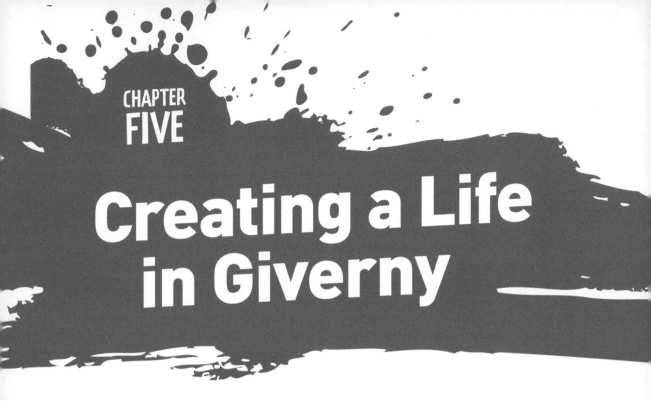

CHAPTER FIVE

Creating a Life in Giverny

Though his fellow artists failed to appreciate his work at Belle-Île, Monet embraced his new method of painting the same subject again and again, capturing shifts in the light and weather. Monet brought this technique back to Giverny, where he created dozens of canvases of a new subject—haystacks. In 1890, he came across the giant haystacks built by local farmers while he was on a walk with Suzanne Hoschedé. The cone-shaped mounds of hay standing 20 feet (6.1 m) tall were everywhere in the French countryside and most people took little notice of them—but not Monet. His obsession with the structures reflected his fascination with the colors,

shadows, and natural beauty of the haystacks. Suzanne became an unwitting participant in Monet's sudden inspiration that day and was asked to fetch his easel and two canvases.

As Monet recalled the story, by the time Suzanne returned, "I noticed that the light had changed. I said to [her], 'Would you go back to the house, please, and bring me another canvas?' She brought it to me, but very soon the light had changed again. 'One more!' and, 'One more still!'"[54] Monet created 30 paintings in the *Haystacks* series, also known as *Wheatstacks* or *Grainstacks*.

For the rest of Monet's career, he would nearly exclusively focus his

A summer morning provided Monet with inspiration for Haystack, End of Summer's warm tones of yellow and orange.

efforts on painting five subjects over and over, each with subtle variations due to the effects of the sun, weather, or other atmospheric conditions: haystacks, poplars, the Rouen Cathedral in Normandy, buildings along the Thames River in London, and his garden pond in Giverny.

Monet often referred to what he called "the envelope" in correspondences. The envelope was Monet's term for seeing the momentary blend of light, atmospheric haze, and other weather conditions as a single unit. This entity enveloped, or covered, a subject for an instant. This might mean that a fine mist in the air blocked out the view of distant objects or a crisp winter air allowed the sun to shine brightly on a haystack. Throughout the 1890s, Monet was passionate in his pursuit of the envelope. He felt this aspect of painting had been ignored by other artists who were more concerned with accurate depictions of people and things.

Whether or not art collectors understood Monet's envelope, they were

In Haystacks, Effect of Snow and Sun, *Monet used cooler blue tones.*

astounded by his haystacks. In April 1891, the demand for the 15 canvases Monet had painted over the winter was remarkable, with offers of 5,000 to 6,000 francs for each painting.

A New Obsession

Monet eventually painted a total of 30 haystack paintings. Even before his Paris exhibition of the *Haystacks* began, however, he was at work on his next series: the poplars along the Epte River. Monet painted these tall trees as he observed them in different climatic conditions and seasons. As with the haystacks, the artist painted the same subjects repeatedly, sometimes waiting for hours or days for the exact moment that he wished to capture on canvas.

In style and color, however, the new paintings were quite different from the *Haystacks* series. While Monet

Monet's Poplars *paintings astonished Paris critics because of their freshness and unique effects.*

Inspired by Poplars

The graceful composition and colors of Monet's *Poplar* series inspired art critic Clément Janin to describe the canvases in poetic terms in an 1892 exhibition review published in *L'Estafette*:

What is it? Not much. Three or four poplars on the edge of a marsh. Their trunks are reflected in the water, the hair of their heads quivers in the sky; farther away, other poplars recede along the road. This is repeated fifteen times, at all hours of the day, with all the variations in appearance brought to things by changes in the surrounding atmosphere and light; here, the clear sweet song of the end of a summer day, before night falls but when already the sky is becoming like watered silk and [an anxious shimmer] of light amethyst and turquoise disturbs the cerulean [blue] serenity of the horizon; there, in the fierce depths of the infinite, gather the dark shades of lapis lazuli through which the rays of sun are concentrated and burn; elsewhere, like pink sailing boats on Oriental seas, fragile clouds driven by the evening breeze, flow pink against a sky of forget-me-nots, and everywhere the poplars sleep, breathe, and murmur, lifting up their supple trunks, mingling their [unfolding beauty], living their own lives within that great collective life of nature.[1]

1. Quoted in Robert Gordon and Andrew Forge, *Monet*. New York, NY: Harry N. Abrams, 1985, p. 167.

painted the haystacks from a distance, he observed the poplars from his studio boat low in the water, painting the slender tree trunks jutting up to fill the tops of the canvases with shimmering color. In addition, the shadows and light reflected off the river are rendered in heightened contrast, with sharp divisions between the blues and yellows, the purples and oranges. Monet created a graceful S-curve of trees, and sweeping arches of foliage move down the canvases from the foreground to the distance.

Like Monet's previous series, the names of individual paintings were simply functional: *Poplars Along the Epte River (Autumn)*, *Poplars Along the Epte River (Sunset Effect)*, and *Poplars Along the Epte River (Dusk)*. Once again, the paintings astonished the Paris art world. When 15 of the 24 paintings were exhibited at the Durand-Ruel Gallery in March 1892, one of Monet's close friends, novelist and playwright Octave Mirbeau, succinctly expressed the public's attitude in a letter to the artist:

It is an absolutely magnificent work ... I felt complete joy, an emotion that I can't express ... The beauty of those lines, the newness of those lines and their grandeur, and the immensity of the sky and the thrill of it all ... you hear me, my dear Monet, never, never has an artist expressed such things, and it is again a revelation of a new Monet ... I am overwhelmed.[55]

Collectors were also overwhelmed, and many of the 15 canvases were sold even before the exhibition began. Others sold in a matter of days.

A Rainbow of Facades

By the time the *Poplar* series was attracting such positive attention, Monet was living in a room above a shop on the Rue Grand-Pont in Rouen, Normandy. He had rented the room to observe the facade of the ancient Rouen Cathedral, marked by spiraling towers and lacy Gothic stonework. Original construction on the cathedral began in the 13th century, and it was added to over the years. For Monet, painting a series of pictures of a building was a departure from the nature canvases he had been creating for more than 10 years. Additionally, this new series, unlike the poplars, was not completed in a matter of months. The artist worked on the canvases in early 1892 before taking a break for about a year. During the time away from his canvases, Monet married his longtime girlfriend, Alice Hoschedé, on July 16, 1892.

Monet resumed painting the Rouen Cathedral in the spring of 1893, and he worked on the paintings in his home studio for another year. The artist had never worked on a single motif, or design, for such an extended period, especially an architectural subject. The result of his efforts was a series of 30 canvases including *Rouen Cathedral, Façade (Gray Day)*; *Rouen Cathedral, Façade (Morning Effect)*; and *Rouen Cathedral, the Façade in Sunlight*.

Journalist Georges Clemenceau divided the *Rouen Cathedral* paintings into four general categories: the gray series, the white series, the rainbow series, and the blue series. Writing in *La Justice*, Clemenceau explained:

Imagine them aligned ... according to transitions of light: the great black mass in the beginning of the gray series, constantly growing lighter, to the white series, going from the molten light to bursting [colors] that continue and are achieved in the fires of the rainbow series, which subside in the calm of the blue series and fade away in the divine mist of azure.[56]

Monet did not exhibit the *Rouen Cathedral* series until May 1895, his first show in three years. By this time, anticipation was high, and the exhibition caused a great sensation marked by both high praise and unkind

Subtle changes in color and shadows separate the many Rouen Cathedral *paintings from one another. Shown here is* Rouen Cathedral: The Portal (Sunlight), *which was painted in 1894.*

criticism. Several reviewers complained that Monet's colors were unrealistic and the lack of details made the canvases seem unfinished. However, congratulations came from an unlikely source: Monet's fellow Impressionists who had been harshly critical of the poplar and haystack canvases. Of the Rouen paintings, Pissarro said he was "carried away by their extraordinary deftness [and] Cézanne ... is in complete agreement."[57]

The Creation of a Garden at Giverny

After this string of successes, Monet took time away from his canvases to develop his estate at Giverny. With his expert painter's eye for color, light, and composition, he began transforming the grounds into magnificent gardens, spending long hours paging through seed catalogs and discussing plant specimens with French gardening experts. Monet laid out several acres of raised planters, fertilized flower beds, and trellises that arched over sand paths. A wide variety of flowers from across the globe were planted, and they were coordinated to bloom continuously from early spring until late autumn.

Monet also upgraded a small marshy pond on his property, enlarging it to four times its original size by diverting a small stream from the Epte River. According to his statement on the building permit, the purpose of the expansion was to create a spectacular water garden "for the pleasure of the eye and also for motifs to paint."[58] Other improvements included the construction of a decorative Japanese-style wooden bridge where the stream flowed into the pond. This was surrounded by wisterias, weeping willows, Japanese apple trees, and bamboo. The pond was filled with *nymphéas*, or water lilies, that bloomed all summer. Monet employed a team of gardeners to pick weeds from the bottom of the pond and scoop up algae so the water retained a mirrorlike reflective surface. Monet could afford these projects since his income was now more than 100,000 francs a year. However, as he told one interviewer, "Everything I have earned has gone into these gardens."[59]

A Return to London

Monet did not make many paintings of his gardens, since they did not reach maturity for many years. However, after painting the splendor of nature for so many years, Monet decided to create another architectural series, checking into the luxurious Savoy Hotel in London in September 1899. Monet's room was on the sixth floor and offered a stunning view of the Thames River and south London. Using this room as his base, Monet made 3 extended painting trips to London during the following 3 years, creating nearly 100 canvases of 3 subjects, the Charing Cross Bridge and the Waterloo Bridge across the Thames, and the Houses of Parliament, where the legislature for the United Kingdom conducts

New Inspiration in Water Lilies

Monet used his gardens at Giverny as an artistic muse, or inspiration. In *Monet: Late Paintings of Giverny from the Musée Marmottan*, author, gardener,

Over the last few decades of his life, Monet would continually use his garden at Giverny as a subject for his paintings.

1. Lynn Federle Orr, Paul Hayes Tucker, and Elizabeth Murray, *Monet: Late Paintings of Giverny from the Musée Marmottan*. New Orleans, LA: New Orleans Museum of Art, 1994, p. 55.

and photographer Elizabeth Murray described the beauty of Monet's water lily pond:

Monet created his water-lily garden for beauty. What he found was endless inspiration and tranquility. His greatest passion and challenge was to paint the fleeting quality of light. In his water garden he discovered infinite motifs. The pond was a mirror reflecting each nuance of atmospheric change—a moving cloud, a ripple of wind, a coming storm. It held inverted images of the surrounding landscape [reflected in the water] while simultaneously supporting thousands of floating water flowers. The effect was that of a prism in the light, spreading shimmering shades of precious gold, ruby, amethyst, sapphire, and topaz over the surface of the water. These flowers were like multifaceted jewels on deep green settings of round, floating, palette-shaped leaves. The pond thus became the focal point for Monet, which he treated with reverence, as a personal sanctuary.[1]

business. Monet explained why he took up this unprecedented project: "What I like most of all in London is the fog … Without the fog, London would not be a beautiful city. It's the fog that gives it its magnificent breadth."[60]

London's fog at that time was actually smog, a mixture of fog and air pollution caused by the widespread use of coal. Nevertheless, the thick blanket of fog, the weak sun, and the smothered light created unusual atmospheric conditions found nowhere else in the world. To Monet, this environment provided a beautiful envelope that he layered over the ancient buildings, the industrialism of the trains and traffic on the bridges, the factories in the distance, and the boats on the water. Of all the paintings made in London, those such as *The Houses of Parliament, Sunset* and *Houses of Parliament, Sunlight Effect* are considered the most remarkable.

When Monet finally exhibited 37 pieces of the massive collection of the *London* series masterpieces in 1904, the show was met with universal acclaim. Art historian Gustave Kahn labeled Monet a "master composer of [artistic] symphonies."[61] English artist Wynford Dewhurst noted

The Houses of Parliament, Sunset *is considered among the finest of Monet's London paintings during this time period.*

Monet was "one of the few original members of the Impressionist group who has lived to see the ... complete reversal of the hostile judgment passed upon his canvases by an ill-educated public."[62] Delighted at his triumph, Monet, now 63 years old, returned to his beloved Giverny gardens, which were now so lush and beautiful that they would provide him with artistic inspiration for the rest of his life.

Water Lilies

In between painting trips to London, Monet focused his artistic eye on subjects closer to home, especially the water lilies growing in his pond in Giverny. In 1899, the artist painted 18 canvases of his Japanese bridge arching over hundreds of violet-colored water lilies and framed by a weeping willow and other trees. Some of the paintings are rendered in muted colors that reflect an overcast rainy afternoon. Other paintings are almost too bright in their liberal use of sunbathed colors such as canary yellow, lime green, purple-pink, orange, and fiery red.

The Japanese bridge paintings were undoubtedly influenced by Monet's love of Japanese art prints. However, in the work that followed, Monet dispensed with the bridge completely, painting only the water lilies and reflections in the pond between 1903 and 1908. This was a much more difficult task, as the bridge gave a conventional sense of perspective and depth to the paintings. Successfully capturing the infinitely changing surface of the shimmering water, the irregular shapes of the water lilies, and mirror images of clouds above proved to be difficult even for a master such as Monet. The artist's feelings were revealed in a 1908 letter: "These landscapes of water and reflection have become an obsession. It's quite beyond my powers at my age, and yet I want to succeed in expressing what I feel."[63]

Monet exhibited the first of the water lily paintings in the spring of 1909, and the paintings sold for record amounts. The artist was now a millionaire who used his money to purchase fine suits,

The Water Lily *series comprises numerous paintings,*
and today they are shown in galleries all over the world.

expensive food, and some of the first automobiles in France. He also traveled throughout Europe and built a greenhouse on his property along with a second studio and a darkroom where he pursued his growing interest in photography.

The Death of Alice

Money and fame could not prevent harsh reality from intruding on Monet's well-constructed life. In the spring of 1910, the Seine and Epte rivers overflowed, swamping his beloved gardens and nearly flooding his home. During this period, Alice became very ill and suffered in great pain until her death in May 1911. After his wife's death, the 70-year-old Monet was lost in grief for months and refused to paint. However, at the end of the year, he picked up his brushes once again, finishing 37 canvases he had begun in Venice, Italy, on one of the last vacations he took with Alice.

Monet's work was interrupted once more in 1912 when he suddenly realized he could not see clearly out of his right eye. Doctors told Monet he had developed nuclear cataracts in both eyes. Cataracts create a milky film over the lens of the eye and eventually cause glaucoma, which leads to blindness. Doctors recommended surgery on his right eye. However, the cataract problem seemed to stabilize and he refused the operation.

Although cataracts distort color perception and make it difficult to focus clearly, Monet was spurred to complete new projects before his eyesight failed completely. In 1915, he built a huge new studio, 75 feet by 40 feet (23m by 12 m), with a glass-paneled roof that rose to a height of nearly 50 feet (15 m). After completing this cavernous work space, Monet lined the walls with 19 huge canvas panels that measured 6.5 feet (2 m) high by 14 feet (4 m) wide. The canvases were mounted on easels with wheels that could be moved around the studio and arranged in different combinations.

The Blue Angel

In 1914, Monet suffered more tragedy when his son Jean died at the age of 46. Jean had become increasingly ill with syphilis over the last years of his life and suffered from psychosis. As his mental

Blanche was a student of Monet's. Shown here is Monet's painting In the Woods at Giverny: Blanche Hoschedé at Her Easel with Suzanne Hoschedé Reading.

state became worse, Jean and his wife, Blanche, moved to Giverny to be near Monet.

After Jean's death, Blanche, the second oldest daughter of Ernest and Alice Hoschedé, moved in with Monet, managed his household and became his assistant. Blanche was also a painter in her own right. She first began painting when she was 11 and spent long hours learning from and observing her stepfather as well as Manet. At an early age, she became Monet's student and assistant, a role she returned to after Jean's death.

Mary Mathews Gedo wrote that Blanche's "role in sustaining her beloved stepfather cannot be overstated."[64] Blanche accompanied Monet on his visits to the home of Georges Clemenceau, at this time a former prime minister, in Saint-Vincent-sur-Jard. She painted his home, gardens, and the sea, and, as a young woman, even completed her own version of Monet's famous haystack paintings. At times it is difficult to tell paintings by the two artists apart—Blanche often used her stepfather's palette, brushes, paint, and canvases.

Clemenceau called Blanche "the blue angel" for assisting her stepfather in his creative endeavors in his final years. As Gedo wrote of her devotion,

During Monet's final years, his stepdaughter (and daughter-in-law) Blanche Hoschedé Monet sacrificed her own artistic interests to devote herself completely to the elderly widower's welfare. The creative paralysis that had gripped the artist from the time of Alice Monet's death in 1911 ended when the death of Blanche's husband, Jean Monet, permitted her to commit herself to stay at the elderly master's side throughout the remaining years of his life.[65]

Blanche relaunched her own career after Monet's death and had her own solo show in 1931 at Galerie Bernheim-Jeune in Paris.

Large Decorations

For several years after Alice and Jean's deaths, Monet worked on a series of 40 massive paintings he called *Grandes Décorations*, or *Large Decorations*. These massive works focused on the light and atmosphere reflected in his lily pond. Four of the panels, simply called *The Morning*, show lilies opening in the glittering light, display-

Visitors viewing the Grandes Décorations at the Musée l'Orangerie in Paris would feel encompassed by the giant water lily paintings all around the room where they are housed.

ing bright flowers over muted planes of water and floating leaves. *Green Reflections* shows the pond in the cool, refreshing shade of late afternoon, and *Sunset* renders the pond in the failing light.

The *Grandes Décorations* paintings, with their built-up crusts of multicolored paint layered onto canvases of immense scale with large brushes, were unlike anything Monet had ever attempted. Thick, pitted areas of pigment contrasted with thin, delicate sections of color, with dark shadows set against intense highlights. In the pursuit of perfection, Monet relentlessly rearranged the order of the canvases. When new paintings were placed together, he scraped off pigment and repainted and revised the pictures so they would

Cataracts and Perception of Color

Monet was first diagnosed with nuclear cataracts in both eyes in 1912, at the age of 72. However, his visual problems began seven years earlier when he began to experience changes in his color perception. On its website, the Vision and Aging Lab at the University of Calgary explained how cataracts caused Monet to see distorted colors that were then committed to canvas by the artist:

> Soon after 1905 (age 65) he began to experience changes in his perception of color. He no longer perceived colors with the same intensity. Indeed his paintings showed a change in the whites and greens and blues, with a shift towards "muddier" yellow and purple tones. After 1915, his paintings became much more abstract, with an even more pronounced color shift from blue-green to red-yellow. He complained of perceiving reds as muddy, dull pinks, and other objects as yellow. These changes are consistent with the visual effects of cataracts. Nuclear cataracts absorb light, desaturate colors, and make the world appear more yellow.

> Monet was both troubled and intrigued by the effects of his declining vision, as he reacted to the foggy, impressionistic personal world that he was famous for painting. In a [1922] letter to his friend G. or J. Bernheim-Jeune he wrote, "To think I was getting on so well, more absorbed than I've ever been and expecting to achieve something, but … my poor eyesight makes me see everything in a complete fog. It's very beautiful all the same and it's this which I'd love to have been able to convey. All in all, I am very unhappy."[1]

1. "Monet, Claude Oscar (1840–1926)," University of Calgary, accessed on April 11, 2018. psych.ucalgary.ca/PACE/VA-Lab/AVDE-Website/Monet.html.

merge with one another. By creating a series in this manner, Monet drew upon his more than seven decades of experience to create timeless, and priceless, works of splendor. When news of his unprecedented works and his huge new studio were described in the press, the road to Giverny was filled with artists and admirers making the pilgrimage from Paris to meet the great painter.

Monet's Last Act

In November 1923, with the *Grandes Décorations* nearly finished, Monet's eye doctor informed him he was blind in his right eye and had only 10 percent sight in his left. The following January,

Monet finally underwent surgery to remove the cataract in his right eye. Two more operations were required in July 1924, and the artist's eyesight was partially restored. By this time, the Musée de l'Orangerie in Paris was set to honor Monet by hanging 22 of the panels from *Grandes Décorations* in 2 oval-shaped rooms. The panels in the first room would reflect the changing effects of light on the lily pond from morning until sunset. The murals in the second room would consist of a panoramic view of the pond as seen through the drooping foliage of weeping willows.

Monet's *Water Lilies* exhibit was set to open on May 16, 1927, but during the winter of 1926 the artist became gravely ill, suffering from a lung tumor that led to a condition called pulmonary sclerosis. On December 5, 1926, Monet died around 1 p.m. Blanche was sitting at Monet's bedside at the time of his death. Three days later, the artist was buried without religious ceremony beside Alice in the family plot in Giverny.

A New Way of Viewing Old Art

In 2018, the National Gallery in London, England, held an exhibition called "Monet & Architecture," which featured 75 of Monet's paintings from different periods. Richard Thomson, guest curator, and Watson Gordon, Professor of Fine Arts at the University of Edinburgh, commented on Monet's use of architecture:

Monet used buildings in his pictures for all sorts of different reasons, primarily pictorial. He could use the regular shape of architecture against the irregularity of nature. Sometimes he used buildings as screens on which the light played. On other occasions, architecture has an almost psychological effect. So, there's a great diversity and range to the way buildings were used in Monet's work.[66]

"Monet & Architecture" was the first Monet exhibition in the United Kingdom in 20 years. It was also the first Monet exhibition of its kind. The artist's landscapes had always been prominently featured, and never before had his work been displayed through the lens of the buildings he painted over his long career. In a review for London's *Evening Standard*, Matthew Collings explains how understated, and yet ultimately clever, the exhibition was: "You could go through the whole thing and not think about architecture. But as soon as you do, you realise how clever the concept is … You are forced to consider subject matter in the work of an artist justly celebrated for transcending it."[67]

Monet Immortalized

The man whose name would eventually become associated with an entire art movement struggled throughout much of his early career. He was often unable to sell his paintings for more than a few hundred dollars and his family went hungry at times.

Unlike many famous artists, however, Monet did know success within his own lifetime, selling some works for tens of thousands of francs so he could pay for his garden utopia at Giverny. Toward the end of his life, he was renowned as a productive artist whose innovative technique pushed and inspired the art world.

Monet would have been astonished to learn some of the price tags that would eventually be attached to his paintings. In November 2016, the sale of one of the paintings in his *Haystack* series sold for a record $81.4 million—$1 million more than the previous record. *Meule*, painted in 1891, was one of the last paintings of the *Haystack* series—one of twenty-five painted between 1890 and 1891—to remain in private hands at the time of its auction. The buyer remained anonymous.

In the years since his death, Monet has become a household name. He was name-dropped in the 1996 teen movie *Clueless*, and the theft of one of his paintings is the centerpiece of the 1999 thriller *The Thomas Crown Affair*. Today, images of Monet's paintings are sold on posters, calendars, T-shirts, and even coffee mugs throughout the world. Monet's name and instantly recognizable Impressionist style have inspired generations of artists and art appreciators worldwide and will likely continue to do so for years to come.

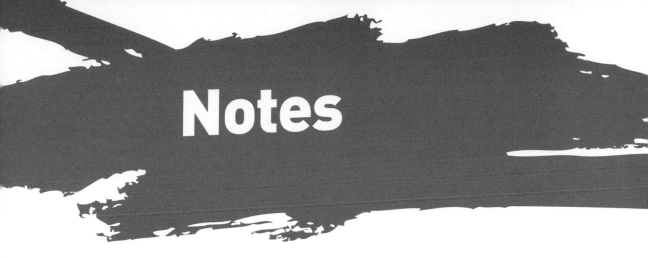

Notes

Introduction: Leading a Movement

1. Quoted in Charles F. Stuckey, *Claude Monet: 1840–1926*. New York, NY: Thames and Hudson, 1995, p. 8.
2. Stuckey, *Claude Monet: 1840–1926*, p. 9.

Chapter One: Childhood in Le Havre

3. Quoted in William C. Seitz, *Claude Monet*. New York, NY: Harry N. Abrams, 1982, p. 11.
4. Quoted in Sue Rose, *The Private Lives of the Impressionists*. New York, NY: HarperCollins, 2006, p. 11.
5. Quoted in Seitz, *Claude Monet*, p. 13.
6. Quoted in Paul Hayes Tucker, *Claude Monet: Life and Art*. New Haven, CT: Yale University Press, 1995, p. 8.
7. Tucker, *Claude Monet: Life and Art*, p. 13.
8. Quoted in Tucker, *Claude Monet: Life and Art*, p. 13.
9. Rose, *Private Lives of the Impressionists*, p. 12.
10. Jim Lane, "The Salon des Refuses," HumanitiesWeb. org, September 20, 1998. www. humanitiesweb.org/human. php?s=g&p=a&a=i&ID=293.
11. Seitz, *Claude Monet*, p. 17.
12. Quoted in "Claude Monet *Luncheon on the Grass*," Musée d'Orsay, accessed on April 1, 2018. www.musee-orsay.fr/en/collections/works-in-focus/search/commentaire_id/ luncheon-on-the-grass-18731. html?no_cache=1.

Chapter Two: Introduction of a Muse

13. Rose, *The Private Lives of the Impressionists*, pp. 44–45.
14. Vanessa Potts, *Monet*. Bath, UK: Parragon, 2001, p. 28.
15. Quoted in Linda Nochlin, *Style and Civilization: Realism*. New York, NY: Penguin Books, 1990.

16. Claude Monet, *Monet by Himself,* ed. Richard Kendall. Boston, MA: Bulfinch, 1989, p. 25.

17. "Claude Monet: The Luncheon (Le Déjeuner), 1868/69," Städel Museum, accessed on April 4, 2018. www.staedelmuseum.de/en/collection/luncheon-le-dejeuner-186869.

18. Jean-Paul Crespelle, *Monet.* London, UK: Studio Editions, 1993, p. 13.

19. Monet, *Monet by Himself,* p. 26.

20. Monet, *Monet by Himself,* p. 26.

21. Sophie Monneret, *Monet: His Life and Complete Works.* Barcelona, Spain: Longview, 1995, p. 36.

22. Monet, *Monet by Himself,* p. 27.

23. Quoted in Crespelle, *Monet,* p. 14.

Chapter Three: Argenteuil and Retreat from War

24. Mary Mathews Gedo, *Monet and His Muse: Camille Monet in the Artist's Life.* Chicago, IL: The University of Chicago Press, 2010, p.104–105.

25. Tucker, *Claude Monet: Life and Art,* p. 48.

26. John Piper, *British Romantic Artists.* London, UK: Collins, 1946, p. 17.

27. Quoted in Tucker, *Claude Monet: Life and Art,* p. 49.

28. Paul Hayes Tucker, *The Impressionists at Argenteuil.* Washington, DC: National Gallery of Art, 2000, p. 21.

29. Tucker, *Claude Monet: Life and Art,* p. 55.

30. Don Morrison, "Monet's Love Affair with Japanese Art," *TIME,* January 4, 2007. www.time.com/time/magazine/article/0,9171,1573 943-2,00.html.

31. Quoted in Charles F. Stuckey, ed., *Monet: A Retrospective.* New York, NY: Park Lane, pp. 58–59.

32. Quoted in Tucker, *Claude Monet: Life and Art,* p. 77.

33. Quoted in Stuckey, *Monet: A Retrospective,* p. 57.

34. Monneret, *Monet: His Life and Complete Works,* pp. 56–57.

Chapter Four: A New Level of Success

35. Monet, *Monet by Himself,* p. 31.

36. Quoted in Gedo, *Monet and His Muse,* p. 200.

37. Quoted in Gedo, *Monet and His Muse,* p. 200.

38. Potts, *Monet,* p. 108.

39. Quoted in Phyllis Marie Jensen, *Artist Emily Carr and the Spirit of the Land: A Jungian Portrait.* London, UK: Routledge, 2016, p. 140.

40. Robert L. Herbert, *Monet on the Normandy Coast.* New Haven,

CT: Yale University Press, 1994, p. 39.

41. Herbert, *Monet on the Normandy Coast*, p. 43.

42. Tucker, *Claude Monet: Life and Art*, p. 115.

43. Monet, *Monet by Himself*, p. 115.

44. Quoted in Crespelle, *Monet*, p. 112.

45. Quoted in Metropolitan Museum of Art, *Monet's Years at Giverny: Beyond Impressionism*. New York, NY: Harry N. Abrams, 1978, pp. 15–16.

46. Quoted in Crespelle, *Monet*, p. 31.

47. Quoted in "Claude Monet: Painting Bordighera in the Riviera Italy," intermonet.com, September 30, 2006. www.intermonet.com/ocuvre/bordig.htm.

48. Quoted in Stuckey, *Monet: A Retrospective*, p. 210.

49. Quoted in "Claude Monet: *The Rocks at Belle-Île, The Wild Coast*," Musée d'Orsay, accessed on April 10, 2018. www.musee-orsay.fr/en/collections/works-in-focus/painting/commentaire_id/the-rocks-at-belle-ile-the-wild-coast-10893.html?tx_commentaire_pi1%5BpidLi%5D=509&tx_comementaire_pi1%5Bfrom%5D=841&cHash=bc857dcfee.

50. Potts, *Monet*, p. 154.

51. "Claude Monet: *The Rocks at Belle-Île, The Wild Coast*."

52. Quoted in Stuckey, *Monet: A Retrospective*, p. 128.

53. Quoted in Tucker, *Claude Monet: Life and Art*, p. 133.

Chapter Five:
Creating a Life in Giverny

54. Quoted in Tucker, *Claude Monet: Life and Art*, p. 141.

55. Quoted in Robert Gordon and Andrew Forge, *Monet*. New York, NY: Harry N. Abrams, 1985, p. 167.

56. Quoted in Stuckey, *Monet: A Retrospective*, pp. 179–180.

57. Quoted in Paul Hayes Tucker, *Monet in the '90s*. New Haven, CT: Yale University Press, 1989, p. 143.

58. Quoted in Tucker, *Monet in the '90s*, p. 255.

59. Quoted in Lynn Federle Orr, Paul Hayes Tucker, and Elizabeth Murray, *Monet: Late Paintings of Giverny from the Musée Marmottan*. New Orleans, LA: New Orleans Museum of Art, 1994, p. 32.

60. Quoted in Tucker, *Monet in the '90s*, p. 244.

61. Tucker, *Claude Monet: Life and Art*, p. 168.

62. Quoted in Stuckey, *Monet: A Retrospective*, p. 226.

63. Quoted in Tucker, *Claude Monet: Life and Art*, p. 187.

64. Gedo, *Monet and His Muse*, p. 228.
65. Gedo, *Monet and His Muse*, p. 6.
66. Quoted in Mark Armstrong, "New Monet Exhibition in London Explores the Use of Buildings in His Work," Euronews, April 10, 2018. www.euronews.com/2018/04/10/new-monet-exhibition-in-london-explores-the-use-of-buildings-in-his-work.
67. Matthew Collings, "Monet and Architecture Review: Magnificent Show Finds a Revolutionary Power in Bricks and Mortar," *Evening Standard*, April 5, 2018. www.standard.co.uk/go/london/arts/monet-and-architecture-review-magnificent-show-finds-a-revolutionary-power-in-bricks-and-mortar-a3806431.html.

For More Information

Books

Brodskaia, Nathalia, and Nina Kalitina. *Claude Monet.* New York, NY: Parkstone Press International, 2011.
> This book explores the challenges Monet faced while creating his masterful works of art.

King, Ross. *Mad Enchantment: Claude Monet and the Painting of the Water Lilies.* New York, NY: Bloomsbury, 2017.
> King's book details the story behind the creation of the water lily paintings and the effects of war and old age on Monet.

Pappworth, Sara. *The Life and Art of Claude Monet.* New York, NY: Rosen Publishing, 2017.
> Pappworth's book gives a closer look at Monet's life and features a sampling of his most famous works.

Shackelford, George T. M. *Monet: The Early Years.* New Haven, CT: Yale University Press, 2016.
> This book is a comprehensive catalog of Monet's early paintings accompanied by essays about his life and influences.

Stamford, Tasha. *Monet.* Broomall, PA: Mason Crest, 2016.
> Stamford's book examines some of Monet's most famous works with additional analysis, historical background, and biographical details.

Websites

Claude Monet

www.marmottan.fr/uk/Claude_Monet_-musee-2517

> The Marmottan possesses the largest collection of Monet paintings in the world. The museum's website provides details about Monet as well as dozens of other impressionists including Degas, Manet, Pissarro, and Renoir.

Claude Monet Biography

www.biography.com/people/claude-monet-9411771

> This website provides an overview of Monet's life as well as a video about his artwork and history.

Claude Monet (1840–1926)

www.metmuseum.org/toah/hd/cmon/hd_cmon.htm

> The website of the Metropolitan Museum of Art in New York City has information about Monet's life as well as his paintings.

Fondation Claude Monet

fondation-monet.com/en/

> Take a virtual tour of Monet's home in Giverny, France, and learn more about the artist, his paintings, and his love of gardening.

Monet, Claude

www.nga.gov/collection/artist-info.1726.html

> This website has biographical information about Monet and details about his paintings on view at the National Gallery of Art in Washington, D.C.

Index

Picture Credits

Cover (screen image) Rawpixel.com/Shutterstock.com; cover (main image) DEA PICTURE LIBRARY/De Agostini Picture Library/Getty Images; pp. 1, 3, 4, 6, 9, 24, 40, 58, 72, 93, 97, 99, 103, 104 (big paint swatch) Lunarus/Shutterstock.com; p. 7 Everett Historical/Shutterstock.com; p. 10 The Art Institute of Chicago/Art Resource, NY; p. 12 Laurent Lecat/Electa/Mondadori Portfolio via Getty Images; pp. 12, 33, 46, 50, 80 (paint caption background) Jaroslav Machacek/Shutterstock.com; pp. 14–15 Private Collection/Bridgeman Images; pp. 20–21 Kimbell Art Museum, Fort Worth, Texas, USA/Bridgeman Images; pp. 22, 29, 49 Fine Art Images/Heritage Images/Getty Images; pp. 25, 27, 33, 34–35, 41, 78 DeAgostini/Getty Images; pp. 36–37, 75 H. O. Havemeyer Collection, Bequest of Mrs. H. O. Havemeyer, 1929/The Metropolitan Museum of Art of New York; p. 38 Yale University Art Gallery; pp. 42–43 Claude Monet/Getty Images; p. 44 Art Collection 3/Alamy Stock Photo; p. 46 Bavarian State Painting Collections/Neue Pinakothek Munich; p. 48 Gift of Sara Lee Corporation, 2000/The Metropolitan Museum of Art of New York; p. 50 Paul Fearn/Alamy Stock Photo; pp. 52, 66–67, 74 VCG Wilson/Corbis via Getty Images; p. 55 1951 Purchase Fund/Museum of Fine Arts Boston; p. 59 Imagno/Getty Images; p. 61 Musee de la Ville de Paris, Musee du Petit-Palais, France/Bridgeman Images; p. 64 The National Gallery of Scotland via Getty Images; p. 70–71 Musee d'Orsay, Paris, France/Bridgeman Images; p. 73 Christophel Fine Art/UIG via Getty Images; p. 80 George Rinhart/Corbis via Getty Images; pp. 82–83 Private Collection/Photo © Christie's Images/Bridgeman Images; pp. 84–85 Leemage/Corbis via Getty Images; pp. 86–87 Courtesy of Los Angeles County Museum of Art; pp. 88–89 EQRoy/Shutterstock.com; back cover vector illustration/Shutterstock.com.

About the Author

Danielle Haynes lives near Dallas, Texas, but spent several years in Buffalo, New York, where she studied English and art history. She has more than 10 years of experience in journalism, both as a writer and editor. When she is not writing, Danielle is reading, watching every movie she can get her hands on, or carrying out a quest to find the best barbecue restaurant in Texas.